BRAINWASHING
AND OTHER FORMS OF
MIND CONTROL

BY MARGARET O. HYDE

79062

McGRAW-HILL BOOK COMPANY

NEW YORK • ST. LOUIS • SAN FRANCISCO • AUCKLAND
BOGOTÁ • DÜSSELDORF • JOHANNESBURG • LONDON
MADRID • MEXICO • MONTREAL • NEW DELHI • PANAMA
PARIS • SÃO PAULO • SINGAPORE • SYDNEY
TOKYO • TORONTO

BRAINWASHING
AND OTHER FORMS OF
MIND CONTROL

Library of Congress Cataloging in Publication Data

Hyde, Margaret Oldroyd, date
  Brainwashing and other forms of mind control.

  Bibliography: p.
  1. Control (Psychology) 2. Brain-washing.
I. Title.
BF632.5.H92   76-55766
ISBN 0-07-031639-2

45MUBP7898

TO FRANCES ERICA HALL

ACKNOWLEDGMENTS

The author wishes to thank the many people who contributed to this book, especially Dr. George W. Albee, Professor of Psychology, University of Vermont; and Dr. Edward S. Marks, Career Counseling Director, Wordsworth Academy, Fort Washington, Pennsylvania.

CONTENTS

1 MIND CONTROL HAS MANY MEANINGS

■ Do you control your mind? Today, most people believe that they are in full control of their own minds and always will be. But there are those who fear the invasion of behavior technology which may manipulate their beliefs through the use of new methods when they are not aware of what is happening. Who controls your mind?

The kind of mind control called brainwashing is frequently in the news. *Brainwashing* is an overworked, imprecise term formerly associated with totalitarian governments and prison camps. Recently, however, cries of brainwashing have come from parents of young people alienated from their families by joining certain religious cults. Brainwashing is a term also used by a wide variety of groups who are concerned generally about maintaining freedom of thought.

The kind of mind control called *behavior modification* is a part of many programs in schools, prisons, and mental hospitals. These projects are designed to predict, control, and modify human behavior, hopefully for the good of the individual and society. Much new work in this area has been stimulated by the increased amount of violence today. While few people argue against the need for help in reducing violence and in preventing crime, many individuals question whether the current behavior modification therapies can accomplish this. Some also question their ethics.

The controversy over the applications of behavior modification as a means of mind control has reached investigations at the federal level as well as local. The interest and concern of both those who approve and those who oppose are helping to make the public aware of the benefits and risks involved in this form of mind control. Definitions of behavior modification vary widely; this appears to be a major reason for the controversy. While psychologists do not include psychosurgery or electroconvulsive shock in their definitions, many writers and other individuals do. One definition of behavior modification might be, "A type of specialized therapy utilizing physical punishment or drug therapy for changing a way of reacting." Another might be, "Any learned response to any stimulus, such as the avoidance of bees after having been stung." Most definitions take a middle road, but behavior modification programs range from those that attempt to change improper eating habits to programs that attempt to restructure violent personalities.

Probably the oldest and most common kind of mind control is that accomplished by drugs, either intentionally or unintentionally. In the United States there are so many billions of prescriptions written for mood-changing drugs each year that we are often called a drug-oriented society. The illegal manufacture and sale of mind drugs is very widespread among both young and old. Many legal mood drugs are not recognized as such by people who depend on them; for instance, the caffeine in coffee, tea, cola drinks, and chocolate is rarely thought of for its stimulating properties. Cigarettes, which contain chemicals such as nicotine that alter mood, are not usually considered in the drug class. Do you think of alcohol as a mind drug? For better or for worse, the tranquilizers, pleasure drugs, prescription stimulants, and other drugs play a major role in the lives of many people. Many books have been written on the subject of mind drugs. See the suggestions for further reading on pages 132–136 for further information in this area.

Mind control courses are being offered to the public on an increasingly wide scale. Perhaps you have friends who have taken courses that they feel enable them to remember better, use ESP, control pain, stop bleeding, or think like Einstein. Reactions to commercial mind control courses vary from praise to criticism. According to some, they can be harmful and are a sort of "inner-peace quickie rip-off."

Consider the wide variety of situations in the news today that involve various forms of mind control. There is the story of a mother who feels strongly that her daughter's allegiance to a cult is a result of brainwashing. The mother persuades some young men to kidnap her daughter from the shopping center where she is peddling candy to make money for a religious cult. Another news article has a picture of a windowless box where a retarded child has been placed from time to time as part of a program claimed to help him progress. In still another news item, one reads of ex-addicts living in a small house that has been compared to a large box. They are going through a program of behavior modification that may help them to be free of their craving for heroin. An adjoining column tells of alcoholics who are attending sessions in behavior therapy to ease the craving for their drug of choice. You might find an ad in the same newspaper for a commercial mind control course that promises wonderful things. Or you might pick up a magazine with an ad for a biofeedback device claimed to help control high blood pressure, improve emotional health, and turn on the power of the mind. Certainly, mind control is in the news in both popular and scientific publications.

Biofeedback has produced some very interesting

results when used scientifically by scientists and doctors in their laboratories at medical centers. Complicated and precise instruments show that many involuntary processes in the body can be controlled voluntarily by a person who has learned this special form of mind control. Only a relatively small number of people use this type of biofeedback, but the numbers who have learned to change the rates of body processes through the form of mind control known as *meditation* run well into the hundreds of thousands. Alpha waves, once a term rarely heard, is now part of the vocabulary of many children.

How can you put mind control to use? Might others "program" you to accept their wills without your being aware of what is happening to you?

Whether or not you want it to be, mind control is here today and is having its effect on the brain that lies quietly in your head. It has been used for centuries by dictators who have held their followers through various types of verbal and physical mind control. Mind control means many things and does many things. Are they good or bad? This question can only be answered if one examines the motives, the methods, and the results. For all who want to understand something about certain kinds of mind control, knowing something about what is in the human head is important.

2 MINDS, BRAINS, AND BEHAVIOR

■ For thousands of years, people have been mystified by the workings of the brain, that three-pound, soft mass of pinkish-gray tissue enclosed in the bony protection of the skull, and resembling an oversized walnut with its convoluted surface. The appearance of this remarkable and complex organ gives no clue to its function.

In ancient times, as long ago as 1700 B.C., the Egyptians recognized that head injuries could cause blindness or lameness, and they did some rather sophisticated neurosurgery. But for many centuries after the Egyptians connected head injuries to physical problems, people did not realize the importance of the brain. They thought that behavior and emotions were controlled by other organs, such as the liver and heart. In the fourth century B.C., Plato concluded that the brain was responsible for man's ability to reason, but he attributed emotions to different parts of the body. Hippocrates, the father of modern medicine, was born shortly before Plato. He was the first to realize that the brain controls all our feelings, thoughts, behavior, and perceptions. Aristotle, a pupil of Plato's, believed that the brain cooled the blood.

The Greek physician Galen, who was born in A.D. 130, made further progress in discovering how the brain and other parts of the nervous system work. From his studies of anatomy and from his experiments on animals, he proved the existence of two kinds of nerve pathways, *sensory* and *motor*. These pathways are functioning all the time in your body. For example, if you step on a sharp stone, you withdraw your foot automatically. Sensory nerves carry the message of pain, causing motor nerves to flash their commands to appropriate muscles, which in turn jerk your foot away. Although Galen was correct in identifying the two kinds of nerves, he believed that the nervous system was hollow and contained a gaseous substance called animal spirits, manufactured by the brain and transmitted through the nerves. For the next fifteen hundred years, the theory of animal spirits remained unquestioned.

Not until the end of the eighteenth century did scientists begin to follow the right track, which eventually led to demonstrable proof that transmission of nerve impulses depends not on animal spirits, but on electrical and chemical changes in the nerves. Most of our present knowledge about the nervous system has been accumulated only in the last three hundred years, since that discovery.

The human brain is so complex that it has been likened to a computer; but, compared to the pathways in the brain, the intricate circuitry of a computer is easy to understand. The memory bank of a computer can be located precisely and all its operations traced. But where in the human brain does memory reside? The answer to that question is not entirely clear, although researchers have discovered that certain specific areas of the brain seem to be responsible for memory.

Mapping of the brain has been possible by various means. During brain surgery on epileptic patients, the famous Canadian neurosurgeon Wilder Penfield discovered that stimulation of brain tissue in certain places aroused the recall of forgotten memories. When different areas were probed, the people described seeing bright, flashing lights. Because brain tissue itself is not sensitive, the people being operated on were awake and felt no pain during the procedure.

The study of people who have suffered brain injuries that involved destruction of different parts of the brain has also helped scientists to localize the functions of the brain. Hardly anyone now takes seriously the preposterous claims of Francis Gall, who in the

1800s popularized the pseudo-science of *phrenology*, or the analysis of bumps on the skull. Phrenology assigns qualities like "amativeness," "wit," and "sublimity" to various parts of the head. However, in the middle of the nineteenth century, a surgeon named Pierre Paul Broca treated a patient who had suffered a stroke and consequently had great difficulty speaking. After his death an autopsy was performed, and a scar was found in the brain. After later finding brain damage in the same place in the brain of another stroke victim who had experienced similar trouble with his speech, Broca concluded that there was a special area that controls speech. Later experiments with animals by others demonstrated that the functions of other parts of the brain could be mapped as well.

Studying animal brains, from the most primitive to the most highly developed, scientists have observed that the later in evolution the animal was developed, the more complex was its brain; human beings have the most highly developed brains. Some primitive animals, such as starfish, have managed to survive as a species for millions upon millions of years without any brains at all, though they have a simple network of nerves. As evolution proceeded, and new forms of life developed, nervous systems became more highly organized. If you had been living when dinosaurs ruled the earth about 150 million years ago, you might have thought that the first mammals that appeared during that era could not possibly survive in competition with meat-eaters like *Tyrannosaurus rex*, who was forty-five feet long. Although the dinosaurs were endowed with gigantic size and terrifying teeth and claws, their brains were sadly lacking. The ten-ton *Stegosaurus* had a brain that probably weighed about two ounces; the nerve bundle in its rear end was larger than its brain. On the other hand, the mammals that appeared about 200 million years ago, when the age of the dinosaurs was dawning, were equipped with better brains.

If you were to compare the brains of a fish and a reptile with some mammalian brains, you would notice that the part of the brain called the cerebral cortex is much larger in the mammals. Some mammals, like the rat, have a smooth cortex. The human cortex, the most highly developed of all, is folded and crumpled so that its large area can fit inside the skull. It is the convoluted surface of the cerebral cortex covering the rest of the brain that has prompted its comparison to an oversize walnut, cleft down the middle and divided into two hemispheres. The human cerebral cortex is responsible for many of the functions that make human beings special among the other animals. Here are the centers that enable you to think, to reason, and to use language. This is the part of the brain that plays such an important part in many kinds of mind control.

Complicated as the human brain is, it is basically an

enlarged extension at the top end of the spinal cord. The spinal cord, as you may know, is enclosed within the vertebral column or backbone, and sends pairs of nerves out all along its length, through openings in the vertebrae. These nerves are both sensory and motor, and reach all parts of the body. In addition to the sensory and motor nerves, the spinal cord also contains nerves that carry messages up and down its length, to and from the brain.

Many kinds of mind control involve reflex actions. The three-inch extension, known as the brain stem, at the top of the spinal cord lies inside the skull along with the other parts of the brain. This very important structure controls many reflex functions that are carried on automatically. For instance, it controls the activity of the digestive system, the heart, and lungs. Although you may be aware of your breathing and you can control it to some extent, it is nevertheless an automatic function. It continues while you sleep without any conscious awareness or effort on your part. If you try to hold your breath, you can do so voluntarily, but at one point the automatic control takes over, in order to insure that your tissues obtain enough oxygen. The brain stem also contains complicated mechanisms that are concerned with your level of awareness (important in many mind control programs) and that control sleep rhythms and dreaming.

Imagine how confusing it would be if every sound, every sight, and all your bodily sensations received equal attention in your mind. Bombardment by all these sensory impressions would undoubtedly prevent you from concentrating on any one activity. However, a part of your brain allows only the important signals to enter into your consciousness. The so-called reticular formation or reticular activating system (RAS) located in this area acts as a kind of filter or monitor for all the messages that your senses receive. Some of these messages are conveyed to higher centers so that they intrude on your awareness, while others are screened out. This is the part of the brain that is probably most affected by drugs and other means of altering levels of consciousness, such as meditation.

When you throw a ball, a complicated system of muscle action takes place. How do you know which muscles to use? You do not make any conscious choices. There is a structure at the back of the head under the cerebral hemispheres. It is called the cerebellum and its function is to coordinate your muscular activity so that your motions are smooth and precise. Although voluntary movements are initiated in an area of the cerebral cortex, it is the cerebellum that directs these movements. Here again is an example of brain activity that is not under conscious control. The cerebellum "knows" how to coordinate the appropriate muscles in order for you to throw a ball or play the piano, even though you may not know which of your hundreds of muscles to call into action.

Most people know that normal body temperature is

98.6° Fahrenheit or 37° Centigrade. How does your body control this? Here is a form of unconscious mind control. Above the brain stem and lying under the cerebral hemispheres are two small areas of the brain called the thalamus and the hypothalamus. The hypo-thalamus is concerned with regulation of body temperature, eating, and drinking, as well as with sexual behavior and emotions. The thalamus serves as a kind of switchboard or station to which all the sensory information that the body receives is relayed. These sensations are then sent to the higher centers in various parts of the cerebral cortex. Smell is the only sensation that is not relayed through the thalamus, but has its own direct connections to the cerebral cortex. In lower animals, like the alligator, most of the cerebral cortex is concerned with the sense of smell because of its importance for survival. Although in humans this so-called "smell brain" does not usually serve an important function for survival, odors can sometimes evoke strong emotional responses. Scientists believe this may be because the brain centers that are concerned with emotions and drives had their origins in this area. Some research has been done that seems to indicate that certain body odors can arouse sexual feelings in people, just as, for instance, a male dog responds to the odor of a female dog in heat.

There are many other parts of the brain in your head that have not been mentioned. For example, the pituitary gland hangs from the hypothalamus by a stalk and sends chemicals into your body that are so important that the pituitary has been called the "master" gland. It triggers reactions of other glands. These reactions may be familiar to those girls and women who use the "pill" as a method of birth control.

Looking at the brain as a combination of three basic units, one finds there are layers of brains. The lowest, and the one in the inside layer, is called the reptilian brain and consists mainly of the brain stem and a part called the midbrain. Above the reptilian brain and, in a manner, fringing the brain stem, is the layer known as the old mammalian brain or limbic system. This limbic system is described as mysterious even by those whose profession is brain research. Without the development of this "emotional brain" in the evolutionary process, mammals might never have progressed beyond the behavior programmed in reptiles. The limbic brain, the thick, doughnut-shaped mass encircling the top of the brain stem, is of special interest to those working with mind control in the area of altered states of consciousness. It is here that stimuli have the effect of mood changing or emotional changes ranging from euphoria to violence. Some organs mentioned earlier, such as all or part of the hypothalamus and a portion of the thalamus, are included in the limbic system, along with other organs.

Surmounting the old mammalian brain is the new mammalian brain, which in man makes up the greater part of the cerebral cortex or thinking part of the brain. The three layers or regions of the brain [as considered from an evolutionary basis] all must work together in an exquisitely and unbelievably complex way day after day.

While there are several types of cells in the brain, the main functions are carried out by nerve cells, or neurons. Their number is so great that it is beyond imagination—at least 13,000 million. These cells use a system of frequency of impulses in each burst which tells the next cell about the strength of the signal. The language of the brain has been compared to a Morse code that uses dots but no dashes. Since each cell can have tens of thousands of terminals on it, one can only wonder at the complexity of the system that enables people to say, "I love you," control the unconscious workings of the human body, and carry on an incredible number of other activities at the same time.

Neuroscience continues to try to unravel the architecture and structure of the human brain, learning more about the chemicals that transmit the messages from one nerve cell to another and about the problems that arise when brain chemistry and structure are abnormal. At the same time, the mind control experts go about their work of trying to make the brain produce behavior for the good or detriment of the body in which it resides.

Many other parts of the brain that have specific functions have not been mentioned since they are more of interest to anatomists and physiologists than those who want to explore the new developments in the world of mind control. The whole brain is so complex and functions in such an incredible way that it outperforms the most sophisticated man-made computers. How it changes ten watts of electricity and some chemicals into thoughts, feelings, memories, dreams, and so on is still largely a mystery. No wonder the control of the mind is possible but far from being completely understood.

3 BEHAVIOR CONTROL: FROM PIGEONS TO PEOPLE

■ A large number of people in today's world are being controlled by a type of behavior modification that is based on early experiments with rats, dogs, worms, pigeons, and other laboratory animals. From laboratory experiments come the principles that alter the behavior of alcoholics, stutterers, violent children, obese adults, bed-wetters, sex offenders, people who fear flying in planes, and a long list of others. While behavior shapers claim a large percentage of successes, critics of their methods call behavior modification a form of thought control that is harsh and soulless.

First consider the beginnings of behavior modification, which go back to the experiments of the early 1900s. Professor E. L. Thorndike of Columbia University is famous for his Laws of Learning, which are based on learning in various animals. An important principle on which the newer theories are based is also one of his, the Law of Effect. This states: "When a modifiable connection between a situation and a response is accompanied or followed by a satisfying state of affairs, that connection's strength is increased: when made and accompanied or followed by an annoying state of affairs, its strength is decreased."

Cats in a puzzle box helped Thorndike to reach the above conclusion. The box was so designed that a cat might escape from it by pressing a button, depressing a lever, or pulling a string. The operation of any one of these devices released a door and enabled the cat to get out.

Thorndike experimented with hungry cats to insure motivation. Food was placed outside the box. When a cat saw the food, it responded in a number of ways. One of these was to claw at the slats across the front of the box. Another was to claw at various wires and attachments used to construct the box. Eventually, the cat would accidentally pull the string, press the button, or make the movement necessary to release the door of the box in which it was placed. Its action was a matter of chance.

Then the cat was put back in the same box. Again, there was a certain amount of clawing and biting, but the escape took less time. With each successive trial there were fewer false and useless moves and the cat's activity was nearer the escape device.

There is a story about one laboratory animal in an

experiment of this type that first operated the releasing device from an upside-down position. When placed back in the box, the animal actually turned upside down again before opening the door.

People generally agree with the Law of Effect that when satisfaction accompanies a response it tends to encourage a renewal of that response. They agree that annoyance accompanying a response tends to discourage its use, or stimulates the substitution of another response that might win a more satisfactory result. However, psychologists and others criticize this law because it does not reveal how the psychological effect that accompanies behavior tends to modify it. The law merely describes the direction of the influence. The behavior modifiers of today are very conscious of the part played by feelings, and their techniques are far more sophisticated than those of Thorndike.

Another individual who played a very important part in the beginnings of behavior modification was the nineteenth-century Russian physiologist I. P. Pavlov. Pavlov was originally more concerned with digestion than with the brain or control of the mind, but he is often mentioned in today's popular mind control courses for his work on behavior changes in animals and people. Pavlov's dog experiments showed how the nervous system controls the flow of digestive juices to the stomach. His work helped to establish the importance of the autonomic nervous system.

Pavlov and his associates worked in a soundproof

room without windows. They observed the actions of their experimental animals through a periscope so as not to distract them.

In one experiment, a dog was placed in a harness. A tube was attached to the duct of the gland that secretes saliva, channeling the saliva to a cylinder that meas·ired exact amounts of flow and time. During the training period, the dog was fed only when placed on the table that held its harness. After the training period, the dog was found to cooperate in the procedure by jumping on the table even before the experimenter commanded it to do so. When the restraining harness was placed on the animal, and when the food appeared, saliva dripped through the tube into the glass measuring device.

In the next experiment, an electric bell was rung just before the food was automatically placed before the dog. Soon, the dog learned to associate the sound of the bell with the food. After a number of times, the sound of the bell alone caused the dog to salivate and lick its chops. Pavlov called this a *conditioned reflex*. Later he showed that stimuli other than the bell could be used in conditioning and he experimented with visual, tactile, and olfactory stimuli as well as the auditory kind. Any response aroused by a stimulus other than the natural one was called a conditioned reflex. Although earlier concepts of connection-forming existed, Pavlov's contribution was important because it placed the facts on an experimental basis and developed a technique in which factors could be accurately measured. His work is considered classic by those who work with behavior changes in laboratory animals and people.

In the bell and food experiment, the dog reacts to the bell as if it were the food. But the important aspect is the fact that the bell *substitutes* for the food and produces a response. There is no association with the bell and the food. Conditioned experiences of all sorts are picked up throughout our lives and affect our personalities.

Although human nature may be much the same for Italians and French, for Asians and Americans, for men and for women, its expression varies widely. No two Italians are alike, even though they may be more alike than an Italian individual and a French individual. Obviously, you are not exactly like your closest neighbor, or friend, or relative, even an identical twin. You are not like anyone else in the whole world, for you are a complex combination of patterns established by many factors in your genetic makeup and environment. Some of the major influences come from conditioning that has been built unconsciously into your personality. These patterns of conditioning are the main keyboard on which the mind controllers play.

While Pavlov experimented with simple inborn reflexes such as salivation, today's behavior shapers have built their techniques to change learned behaviors.

According to some theories, a good part of behavior is based on conditioning. John Watson, an American psychologist, was important in founding the behavioral school of psychology in 1913. This school of thought views humans and other animals as reacting according to the way impulses travel over nerve paths. This way is altered by experience or conditioning.

While no school of psychology uses Watson's name per se at present, he has been called the Freud of behavioristic psychology. His classic study showed how fear may be acquired. In this experiment, a one-year-old child was handed a white rat and the child showed no fear. Then a loud noise was made when the child was given the rat again, and the frightening noise and the rat were soon associated. The child came to fear the rat as well as the noise.

At a time when people believed that heredity and inborn tendencies determined most behavior, Watson insisted that almost all behavior was a product of conditioning. While the importance of heredity has been reasserted, most psychologists still lean toward Watson's views of the primacy of conditioned learning.

The theories of Pavlov and Watson explain one kind of conditioning, known as Pavlovian or classical conditioning. This kind can be illustrated by the following example.

In all normal newborns, when something is brought near the eye, the eye blinks. So when a mild puff of air is directed toward an infant's eye, the eyelid normally closes. In experiments, researchers used a photoelectric device sensitive to the light changes caused by a blinking lid to record such changes on a polygraph.

In one laboratory study, the puff of air was paired with a tone that an infant could hear. After fifty experiences of air puff combined with tone, it was observed that infants blink from the tone alone. Infants as young as ten days were found capable of this learning. It was also noted that those who were incapable of this type of learning had other deficiencies as well.

Conditioned eye blinks in which the tone (the conditioned stimulus) and a puff of air (the unconditioned stimulus) are paired is called *classical conditioning*. This type is used in some behavior modification. The other type of conditioning, known as operant, is based on rewards and punishment for behavior. In operant conditioning, behavior is changed by manipulating the consequences of each act.

Suppose you go to a friend's house for dinner and find that his five German shepherds are in the living room rather than in the kennel where he usually keeps them. Your friend explains that he has been working on a special training program with the dogs. In fact, they are very well behaved.

Before long, he takes four to the kennel and allows one to remain in the living room. While you are eating, the dog leaves the living room and finds its way to your place at the dining room table, where he nudges your arm while you are eating. Obviously, he is asking for some food. Your host remarks that he forgot to feed that dog today and gives this as his reason for keeping the animal in the house. Your host picks up a large piece of meat from his plate and tosses it on the hearth in the dining room. The dog rushes toward it and picks it up, but just as he is about to close his jaws on it, your host calls "Poison!" in a strident tone. The dog immediately drops the meat. Then your host says, "You may eat. The meat is chemically pure." And the dog eats.

You are aware that the dog has been trained to perform a trick for you and if you know something about conditioning, you are not surprised at the explanation. As with the bell and the food, the word "poison" in this case is used as a substitute for punishment. The dog has been conditioned not to eat when it hears the word "poison" given in a certain commanding tone of voice. Rewards for obeying helped to reinforce the correct action during the training period.

Operant conditioning, on which much of behavior modification is based, makes use of consequences to strengthen or weaken behavior. Rewards are given for desired responses and punishments are used to discourage repetition of undesired behavior. This seems quite obvious to most people. One learns to avoid bees after being stung by one. Babies smile at mothers who reward them with pleasant words and hugs when they smile. B. F. Skinner, the famous psychologist, made a science of using operant conditioning on animals in the laboratory. Beginning in the mid-1950s experiments that closely resembled those he developed on animals in the laboratories found their way into mental hospitals. This was years after he began working with the famous "Skinner box," which gives a caged animal an opportunity for reward and/or punishment. Skinner observed that after one of his hungry laboratory rats accidentally stepped on a lever that released food into its cage, it repeated the experience. Soon the rat learned to associate the lever with the reward. From this simple beginning, the controversial and complicated techniques of behavior modification grew into an important influence on the behavior of people. Even the "Skinner box" is so famous that you may pick up a current magazine and find instructions for building one for a hobby or science project.

The behavior modification techniques for both laboratory animals and humans have been called the "carrot and the stick," meaning that one is rewarded for good behavior and/or punished for bad or unwanted behavior. Take a look at some behavior modification in action in a school lunchroom. Keep in mind the parallel between the animal experiments and the behavior therapy applied to people.

The elementary-school lunchroom at Mound Elementary School in Cleveland, Ohio, was typical of many. Children squealed, fought, threw peanut-butter sandwiches at each other, and were generally unruly. Several public-school psychologists and university staff members worked out a plan of behavior modification to end specific kinds of behavior. In order to accomplish this, they trained six local house-wives in the techniques of behavior modification that were to be used to achieve desired results. Rewards and punishments were spelled out, to be used when certain unwanted behavior took place as the children ate. The housewives also made clear to the children the kind of behavior that was target for change.

The children found that throwing a sandwich would result in their being sent off to sit alone in a storeroom until they felt they could control their behavior. If they ate lunch as well-behaved children, they might be rewarded for their good behavior by special privileges such as extra time for movies, gym, or outdoor play. In some lunchrooms in the program, children were given punishments of an old-fashioned variety, such as copying essays or writing an essay that forced accountability by misdeeds.

The combination of the behavior modification techniques of rewards and punishments, plus the essay copying, brought about a 22 percent reduction in the unwanted behaviors considered targets for the program. Behavior modification alone decreased undesirable behavior by 58 percent. The behavior modification technique along with essays forcing verbalization of misdeeds was about 90 percent successful in eliminating unwanted behavior.

After the conclusion of the lunchroom behavioral study, frequency of the target behavior and other misbehavior incidents were tallied by researchers on a daily basis and summarized. Early in 1976 the school principal reported that she felt the program helped students develop a higher degree of self-control more easily and more quickly than pupils did in neighboring schools. She also noted that many studies support the premise that teacher expectancy determines to some degree the frequency of appropriate versus inappropriate student social behaviors. Aides in a behavior modification program where appropriate behavior is rewarded help to increase desired behaviors.

The experiment described above differs from "old-fashioned discipline" in that the behavior to be changed was spelled out, step by step, and so were the rewards and punishments. Another difference is that in behavior modification, positive aspects are stressed, whereas negative aspects are emphasized with old-fashioned techniques.

The experiments in the elementary-school lunchrooms took place in recent years, but as long ago as the late 1930s chimpanzees obtained lunch in a behavior modification program in the laboratory. Grapes were the reward when a chimpanzee placed a chip in a slot, and the action was quickly repeated by the chimps who learned to obtain more rewards by using more chips. They also learned to press a bar to obtain a chip, and to save a number of chips to exchange them for grapes when the experiment showed them this was a profitable kind of behavior. Grapes were called reinforcers, since they reinforced the behavior. In some cases, chimps were taught to lift weights in order to obtain chips that could be used to obtain grapes. Then they learned to lift weights just for chips that they could use to obtain grapes or bananas at a later time.

This technique is called a *token economy*, and it has been applied in many human situations—from children who read for tokens that could be exchanged for candy, cookies, cake, or toys to people in mental hospitals who hoarded tokens that obtained the privilege of doing something the patient especially liked. Token economies have been used in working with retarded children, juvenile delinquents, adults in prisons, adult psychotics, and others. From the laboratory came ideas that could be used to help people in an almost endless number of situations.

A famous experiment that helped in the development of behavior modification techniques was one in which pigeons were taught to play Ping-Pong. Pigeons are good laboratory animals because of their pecking behavior. When a pigeon acted the way a trainer wanted it to act, a reward dropped into a small container. The reward was delivered by a dispenser immediately following the correct behavior, and it was given inconspicuously so that the animals were not distracted by the experimenter. In training for Ping-Pong, a pair of pigeons was placed in a Skinner box and a ball was placed in the middle of the Ping-Pong table. When the ball rolled to one side of the table, the pigeon on that side pecked at the ball, driving it back across the table. A simple reward, such as a food pellet, encouraged this correct behavior. The pigeon on the other side then pecked at the ball and sent it back and was rewarded. Skinner trained pigeons to volley the ball as many as six times before one scored a point by having the partner miss the ball. Other pigeons were trained by this reward method to play a bowling game, to discriminate between colored disks, and to perform a variety of tasks.

Behavior modification has been used to train pigeons to inspect gelatin capsules that contain medication. When time-release capsules are defective because of double caps on them, medication is not released properly in the human body. Inspectors have to watch for imperfections as capsules move along the assembly line before packaging. Working with the fact that capsules with two caps produced two spots of light under certain conditions, scientists trained pigeons to peck three times when they saw a defective capsule. While their work was accurate 99 percent of the time after a training period of one week, the pigeons never inspected other than on an experimental basis because it did not seem practical.

In another experiment, pigeon behavior was directed in such a way that the birds could identify some faulty electronic parts and could apply themselves over a period of time that humans found almost unbearable. Their capacity for work at a task for a four-hour span and their good record of accuracy did not overcome some practical problems, and the use of the birds for industry remained experimental only.

Conditioning people has been much more practical, even though there is much controversy about the ethics of it all. Skinner's theory, developed with laboratory animals, has found its way into an unbelievably wide variety of places. And no matter what the place or what kind of behavior is being modified, the technique still goes back to the basic principles. The following statement is oversimplified, but it does represent the main idea:

> Most behavior is learned, whether good or bad. Learned behavior is influenced by the consequences which follow it. These consequences influence whether or not the particular behavior is repeated.

This is true of the pigeons that were rewarded for playing Ping-Pong, for the rats that pressed levers for food, for the rats that learned to avoid shock, and for students and other people who are under the control of the behavior shapers, whether willing or not. It is also true that psychologists feel that *all* behavior is constantly being modified by its consequences. Behavior modification uses a scientific basis with a statement of goals and a plan to reach those goals. Behavior shapers break this procedure into small steps, recording the events and systematically making changes in the consequences. This is *basically* no different from any social experience where a person decides to spend more time with people who compliment him/her, or avoids people after an unpleasant encounter with them. This is also true of situations that do not involve people. In a sense, behavior modification is always occurring.

Rewards for laboratory animals usually take the form of food. Rewards for people depend on what the individual person likes and on what is practical. In the lunchroom situation mentioned earlier, special privileges such as more gym would not be used if the boy or girl being studied or modified did not like gym. Just as a hungry rat will modify behavior faster because it wants the reward, so will a person change behavior faster if the reward is one that is greatly desired.

Punishment is found to be effective in many situations. In a sense, avoiding punishment might be considered a reward. For example, if a laboratory animal learns that certain behavior will bring punishment, it will be rewarding to the animal to avoid that behavior. When people are trying to do away with undesirable habits, slight electric shocks in laboratories, denial of privileges, and short periods of isolation in school or at home are sometimes used as punishment.

No matter what the variety, behavior modification is

based on the theory that behavior of laboratory animals and people is a result of both genetic codes and learned behaviors. If one alters either of these, behavior will change. Certainly, alteration in the environment is the only approach available, since changing genetic codes is impractical, if not impossible.

Causes of violent behavior are the controversial subject of much discussion; as the amount of violence increases, our knowledge of those causes becomes increasingly important. According to Skinner's followers, one should not put people in roles where their good behavior is not reinforced. In other words, control of environment is all-important. It is not always possible, but if one believes that violence is learned behavior and can be unlearned, steps to prevent or stop it might be helpful.

Consider a laboratory experiment with pigeons on the cause of violence. A pigeon pecks at a disk on the wall of its box and obtains food on a regular schedule. At a certain point in the experiment, the food does not drop into the container from the dispenser when the pigeon pecks at the disk. The pigeon becomes frustrated and attacks a pigeon in a nearby box. This aggressive behavior appears to be due to lack of reinforcement and a change in expectations of the environment.

In some schools and clinics, behavior modification for violent children is based on the theory that violent behavior is learned and can be unlearned. Take the case of Tommy; it is fictitious but follows the general pattern. Tommy is a ten-year-old who disrupts classroom activity by his temper tantrums, which occur at the slightest frustration. At home, Tommy screams, kicks, throws things on the floor or at his sister many times each day. His mother says he has always been violent and has never obeyed her. At the clinic, psychologists study Tommy's behavior and pick out some specific things that they hope to change.

Before putting a program of behavior modification into action, a trained worker from the clinic spends several days at Tommy's home watching the interaction in the family setting. The father has left them, so the mother is busy with her work both outside and inside the home. She has little time to spend with Tommy, but he gains attention by his violence. The attention comes in the form of threats, scolding, shouting, giving in to him when he threatens violence for not getting his way. This kind of attention, even though of poor quality, tends to reinforce the unwanted violence.

Tommy's mother was given a guide to follow in which certain specific, unwanted behaviors were to be punished by short "time out" stays on the stairway with no attention paid to the tantrums. Each one was to be immediate and short rather than the severe long-term punishment formerly attempted. Rewards were to be given for obedience. Tommy's mother was asked to spend several days listing the number of times he disobeyed and the number of times he obeyed. She was surprised to find that he did obey about one-third of the time, but until the list was made she had never noticed or reinforced good behavior. When such consequences were put into effect, Tommy's behavior began to change. After a six-month period, help from the professionals at the clinic was no longer needed. Schoolwork had improved with the cooperation of the teacher, who was also willing to practice some behavior modification techniques.

Operant conditioning techniques have long been used in the laboratory and have been applied to people for many years. Nevertheless, they are still not accepted by many individuals. A school principal might feel that the rewards are a form of bribery, as one did when psychologists tried to introduce programs in his school. A parent replied, "No one ever paid me for being good and no child of mine is going to be paid for being good." This father seemed to feel that rewarding a child was somehow immoral. Actually, the father *was* rewarded for being good since his parents must have approved good behavior and punished bad behavior. And while the theory underlying some of the projects is simple, the environment is not. Administration in a school may not be set up to report good behavior as needed in a behavior modification program.

Much of the furor over behavior modification is based on the use of punishment devices. Trained behavior shapers usually work with positive reinforcements or, if they do use negative consequences, they are not severe. Many cases of cruel treatment have been reported, especially in prisons, mental hospitals, and other confined situations. Such abuses became the subject of an investigation of individual rights and the role of the United States government in behavior modification programs. Many prison experiments have been labeled as trials on humans of theories learned in the laboratories. Most cruel treatment is done by improperly trained staff and *not* by behavior modification–trained professionals. Some of the controversial behavior modification programs are described in the next chapter.

4 BEHAVIOR MODIFICATION: GOOD OR BAD?

■ Because behavior modification is always occurring, it is impossible to answer the question, "Is it good or bad?" What kind of behavior modification is good? What kind is bad? Perhaps you agree with those who feel that any behavior modification in which the subject agrees to cooperate is good, while any in which there is no wish to be changed on the part of the subject is bad.

Consider this example of behavior modification. Peter, age two, is being toilet trained. The process is broken into steps, with appropriate rewards at each step. He is introduced to a doll that wets in a potty and he watches the procedure. Then, he and his teacher pull up the doll's training panties and reward the doll with a tiny piece of cookie. Peter is free to play with the toys that are scattered around the room and from time to time the teacher asks him if he is dry. When he is, he is rewarded with a small cookie. He is placed on the potty at intervals and amply rewarded with praise and food when he uses it for the first time. He is also helped with dressing afterward. When Peter wets his training pants, he helps to clean up the mess and is led to the potty on some practice trips. After he has been successful in the new experience several times, the doll is put away. Eventually, rewards of food and praise are reduced and not given for every success. Peter has learned to announce his readiness to urinate and to experience the reward of knowing he can use the bathroom as adults do rather than wear diapers or have wet training pants.

Mothers of toddlers frequently use a behavior modification technique to train their children to use a potty or the toilet. Learning to discriminate time and place for urination is hastened by the use of immediate rewards. Once the learning has taken place, rewards are used intermittently; they are no longer needed after the other benefits of properly using the bathroom are learned.

Few people, if any, object to use of behavior modification in the above manner. Nor do they complain about its use to help emotionally disturbed children who suffer from autism. Autistic children may be alert when very young, then mentally withdraw into a kind of internal dream world. They no longer speak or respond to the external contact of the outside world. Some mutilate themselves. Many have been condemned to the worst wards institutions have to offer where they have been considered hopeless. Today, a small number are responding to programs such as the education projects for them at some California elementary schools. Here language experts and behavior shapers work together with operant conditioning tuned to the needs of individual children. One child might react to a shout of "No!" followed by loud slaps on a table, while another changes unwanted behavior only after a period of isolation. Children are "trained to the wall" or forced to sit facing the wall, by teachers who restrain them to prevent self-destructive behavior. The children are restrained but they are not held or comforted, so the wall becomes aversive. Only children under nine years of age can be treated this way by most teachers since it is impossible for most adults to hold an older and stronger child when the self-destructive behavior begins. After a time, a simple "No!" usually serves to halt behavior that may consist of biting, screaming, kicking, punching, babbling in a monotone, or other undesirable acts.

Autistic children often have strange eating habits, insisting on a particular kind of food, or even a particular brand of food. This helps in a reward program, for favorite foods can be used as rewards for good behavior. Learning to have eye contact with a teacher, giving some sign of affection, and various forms of self-control that are taken for granted with most children are signs of progress for these children. Obviously, the behavior shapers who work with these children must have a great deal of patience along with their special skills of applying behavior therapy.

One might expect the application of conditioning techniques to the problems of all exceptional children to bring little or no objection from anyone. Some of the most difficult children have been responsive and many have shown tremendous improvement. But punishment and reward systems come under scrutiny, and in some cases punishments are so harsh that there is good reason for concern.

Recently, for example, two teachers in Montana were found to be using a 4½-x-4½-x-3-foot box to confine a retarded child as a means of punishment. The teachers' contracts were not renewed for the following year after the situation was discovered and brought to the attention of authorities. Such cruel and unusual punishment is, hopefully, the exception rather than the rule.

Many teachers report good results with reinforcing good classroom behavior with simple methods. For example, a poor reader who disliked books was encouraged through the use of colored strips of paper. The teacher put six strips of paper on the boy's desk. Each time he read well for a period of time, she removed one of the strips. Actually, this appears to be just the reverse of the gold-star reward technique, which has been so criticized. In this case, the experiment involved making the boy aware that he could read well if he was encouraged. While not everyone agrees with the usefulness of gold stars or simple rewards for small bits of improvements, some behavior modifiers feel that they have a place in encouraging desired behavior.

A great concern of those who disagree with the basic idea of behavior therapy is that it may not accomplish its aims because it does not get to the *source* of the trouble. For instance, some psychiatrists view *phobias* as deep-seated fears that are symptoms of some deeply buried problems. Behavior therapists consider the phobic reaction to be a bad habit that has been learned and can be unlearned.

Consider the case of a person who is so afraid of snakes that s/he will not walk in a field or a park. This may be a problem based on a childhood incident in which the child was frightened by snakes, or it may be a fear that replaced some other problem that was created and buried in the unconscious mind during childhood. A psychoanalyst would try to get at the source of the problem and explore the person's past to see if the original problem could be uncovered. Such therapy might involve a number of visits per week for a period of years. If the fear of snakes is a coverup for another problem, this would be discussed. After it was brought to the surface from the patient's unconscious, it could be better understood and perhaps brought into more normal perspective. The patient could then walk in a field or park without an abnormal fear that a snake might be there.

A psychologist or psychiatrist who uses behavior therapy might approach the problem in a different way. Relatively few people have the time or money for psychoanalytic therapy as described above. Since behavior therapy involves shorter treatment, far greater numbers of people can be helped, even on an individual basis. Behavior therapists hope the public will appreciate the relief from misery which this technique has brought to so many people. They claim that they do deal with the basic anxiety behind the fears.

One method of helping a person through behavior therapy is the use of a technique called *systematic desensitization.* Let's use the example of the snake phobia again. A therapist may ask the person to imagine a harmless snake in a cage in the room. Then, step by step, the person may be introduced to pictures of snakes, to toy snakes that move about in a room, to real snakes that are harmless and present in a cage. The stimulus, such as the snake, is presented repeatedly in small but increasing doses while the patient is relaxed. In this way, the fear can be decreased until it becomes more realistic. Later the person may be able to stroke harmless snakes and hold them in gloved hands. Next, when the person becomes comfortable, s/he may hold a snake in bare hands. At the end of the conditioning procedure, a person could be comfortable in a room with a harmless snake crawling around the floor. S/he might even pick it up and let it crawl freely over his/her lap.

Phobias, or intense fears, take many forms. Some of the more common are fear of height, dogs, cats, dirt, flowers, closed places, elevators, and drowning. Over a hundred phobias are listed at one clinic that helps people to overcome such problems. But no matter what the particular phobia, the person's life is affected by it. There is usually such dread of the particular thing or situation that just thinking about it can make the person feel anxious or unable to move.

A wide variety of treatments have been developed in recent years. Many are based on the systematic desensitization approach described above. It was developed by Joseph Wolpe, a major contributor in the field of behavior therapy. In 1961, this Temple University psychiatrist began using the technique on patients who suffered from various phobias. One of his early patients was a twenty-three-year-old trolley-car driver who suffered from intense reactions at the sight of human blood. He began treatment after the trolley car he was driving hit a woman who walked in front of it. Although the woman was not seriously hurt, she bled considerably in the head area. The driver was so upset by the sight of the blood that he became emotionally disturbed and could no longer function at his job.

Dr. Wolpe found that his patient's phobia went back ten years to the time when his father was killed in an accident. But rather than "work through" the problem stemming from this childhood experience, Wolpe used systematic desensitization to change the man's current reactions to the sight of blood.

Since relaxation is an important part of the systematic desensitization technique, in this case the therapist hypnotized his patient to help him relax. Then Wolpe asked the man to think about blood in a situation that was not frightening. The patient visualized a bloody bandage lying in a basket. Step by step, Wolpe conditioned the man as he led him through imaginary situations involving blood that were more and more anxiety-provoking. Finally, the man could confront the sight of human blood without unusual anxiety.

The relaxation part of this kind of behavior therapy is accomplished by various methods. A therapist might spend several sessions teaching the patient or client how to locate certain muscle groups, tense them, and then relax them. Relaxation is also furthered by teaching breathing techniques. As the person becomes conditioned and can imagine scenes that are more and more vivid, relaxation is accomplished before going from one step to the next.

A behavioral technique that some people consider strong medicine is called *flooding* or implosive therapy. While a person who is being desensitized is asked to master a fear in gradual steps, one who undergoes implosive therapy is put in a position that can be compared to throwing a nonswimmer in deep water.

Suppose a woman is afraid of insects. Her therapist asks her to imagine some insects in the distance. The number of insects grows, and a horde of them is coming closer and closer. The woman who feels terror at the sight of one insect undergoes severe anxiety, but she continues to imagine what her therapist instructs her to think about. She feels insects touching her body. Now they are crawling all over her. The therapist continues in this manner until the woman is exhausted from her severe emotional turmoil. According to theory, she no longer fears the insects. While this kind of conditioning treatment works quickly for some people, its detractors feel that it is a cruel way to overcome a phobia.

Of course, such a method is used only with permission of the patient. The cure is accomplished because the fear of insects is extinguished when the person realizes no real harm is done.

A technique that is even more unpleasant but that brings desired results for some phobic patients or clients* is known as "in vivo flooding." With this technique, the patient is not asked to imagine a feared situation, but is actually put into such a situation, in the presence of the therapist, who helps him/her confront the situation. A person with a terrible fear of flying in a plane might be persuaded to make a trip

*Doctors treat "patients"; many psychologists and other therapists prefer the term "client."

with the therapist. While in flight, the therapist directs the person's attention to the theory of flight, to the relative safety of flight as opposed to other forms of transportation, to the speed of the plane, to the landscape below, to the clouds, and so on.

A more popular technique used by those who apply variations of systematic desensitization to help people overcome their fears is one known as *modeling*, or observational learning. In one experiment, a group of eighteen children of preschool age who feared dogs were separated into two groups, one being used as a control. Nine of the children were shown a film. In it, a boy who was afraid of dogs overcomes his fear and is comfortable petting them. Then all eighteen of the children were asked to pet and feed a large dog. The control group still showed fear, as one would expect. Eight of the nine who saw the film were able to pet the dog and feed it some frankfurters. Dr. Robert Liebert, a psychologist at the State University of New York at Stony Brook, who directed this experiment, reported that the ninth child did pat the dog, but instead of feeding it, he ate the frankfurter himself.

Behavior therapy is being used to treat addictions, too. Addiction may be defined as an obsession, a compelling urge, a thought that keeps returning. If such a definition is used, one might consider a person as being addicted to food, cigarettes, coffee, and alcohol, as well as other drugs. At the phobia clinic of Manhattan's Metropolitan Hospital Center, one of the approaches is aversion therapy. If your addiction is fattening food, for example, you may find yourself viewing slides of delicious-looking food—moist chocolate cake, banana splits, or whatever your favorite fattening foods are. You sit in a special chair and as your mouth waters and/or your hunger increases, a shock makes your fingertips tingle. The shock is harmless but somewhat unpleasant; through it, you learn to associate negative reactions with the foods you normally enjoy. This technique has been successful in helping obese people to avoid foods that they view at the clinic, although the effects last for only about six to twelve months. However, the process can be repeated.

Many people who are addicted to overeating, cigarettes, or alcohol find that they can change their behaviors if they wish to do so through the use of shame therapy. Here, the unwanted behavior is discussed by a group in the presence of the person who has come for help. Their disgust helps to take the reward or reinforcement away from what has been a pleasant habit for the addict.

Applications of behavior modification fill large volumes of books. These describe a wide range of problem situations, techniques, and important advances in theory, research, and practice. It is interesting to note that at times even the professionals express conflicting theories.

One case report in *Behavior Therapy with Children*,

edited by Anthony M. Graziano, describes the use of a simple technique to help Susan, an eleven-year-old girl suffering from insomnia. When her parents were home, Susan would lie awake for about two hours each night before falling asleep. Susan was reluctant to remain at home when her parents went out and would usually lie awake until they returned. On one occasion she left the house and searched the neighborhood for them.

After several interviews and a home observation, a therapist taught Susan to relax at bedtime. She was taught to tense and then relax various muscle groups and a thirty-minute tape recording was made to guide her on future nights. Susan played this for herself and followed the instructions. She was able to fall asleep at the end of the thirty minutes' duration of the tape, if not during it. Susan's mother reported that she was less fatigued during the day. After a two-week period she used another tape recording that eliminated the tensing of muscles but provided instructions for relaxation. After one week with this, a fifteen-minute tape was used each night for another two weeks. As in the case of the other tapes, she usually fell asleep at the end or before the end of the instructions. This mind control, although under the direction of a therapist, was a development of self-control. It also served to alleviate the anxiety she felt at being left alone in her room, since anxiety is incompatible with relaxation responses.

While the term behavior modification is sometimes used in the press to cover psychosurgery, electroconvulsive therapy, and the administration of drugs independent of any special behavior of the person receiving the medication, psychologists object strongly to such usage, noting that behavior modification is based on behavioral techniques. True behavior modification means the following of procedures based on the explicit and systematic application of principles and technology derived from research in experimental psychology.

True behavior modification is neither good nor bad; it is ethically neutral. It can be practiced by people who have unethical goals as well as by those who have the good of the patient or client in mind.

5 BENDING MINDS
BEHIND BARS

■ The ethics of brainwashing people in prisons has been argued about by those in the justice system and by society at large. Feeling ranges from mild protest to uproar over certain programs and techniques. Most controversial has been the question of mind control by surgery resulting in destruction of small amounts of brain tissue.

Attitudes about prisoners' rights also cover a wide range. Professor James V. McConnell, a psychologist at the University of Michigan who is famous for his experiments with flatworms, writes, "I do not believe that the Constitution of the United States gives you the *right* to commit a crime if you want to: therefore the Constitution does not guarantee you the right to maintain inviolable the personality forced on you in the first place—if and when the personality manifests strongly antisocial behavior."

The roots of prison brainwashing go back to 1962 when Professor Edgar Schein, an MIT psychologist, addressed himself to the topic "Man Against Man: Brainwashing." He urged prison officials to begin exploring the techniques used on American POWs during the Korean War, using different goals, such as the rehabilitation of prisoners. Dr. Schein expressed the opinion that in order to produce a marked change of behavior and/or attitude, it is necessary to weaken, undermine, or remove supports to the old patterns of behavior and the old attitudes.

He suggested that one think of brainwashing not in terms of politics, ethics, or morals, but in terms of the deliberate changing of behavior and attitudes by a group of men who have relatively complete control over the environment in which the captive population lives.

Certainly the prison psychologists and psychiatrists, and the prison authorities, have the power to reconstruct the personality of a prisoner. But in the case of behavior modification, the important question appears to be the goal and whether or not the prisoner wants to obtain the goal that will help him/her to realize his/her potential as a contributing member of society. Unfortunately, some programs teach submission to all authority. They do not prepare prisoners to lead more successful lives in the world to which they will return.

Recent court rulings have called attention to possible abuses of the use of positive and negative reinforcement, since it is not clear whether or not prisoners can be true volunteers in any experimental prison program. A prisoner who refuses to participate may feel that this lack of cooperation might be held against her/him at the time of parole, or one who participates might do so hoping for earlier release.

Behavior modification techniques used to help people who are not in institutions are almost always used at the request of the patient or client. When this is the case, there is rarely any controversy. But what about a person in jail where behavior modification is used or abused? Some programs called behavior modification do help both prisoners and the society into which they will be paroled. Other programs appear to be increasing the violence in personalities who are already hostile and aggressive.

In 1974, the Institute of Society, Ethics, and the Life Sciences reported the results of a questionnaire sent to Commissioners of Corrections in fifty states.

Many behavior-shaping methods were common. It was noted that fourteen states use token-economy systems for adult offenders and six states used them for juveniles. Points or tokens were allocated for pro-social behavior, and these could be exchanged for goods or services.

Aversion therapy was reported in use in seven states. The technique was used primarily to treat alcoholics and sexual offenders, and in every case, it was reported that the participant did so on a voluntary basis. However, since parole boards are known to be favorably disposed to prisoners in treatment, the question arises as to how voluntary the participation was. One state reported using a drug, apomorphine, on inmates who had broken prison regulations. The drug induces fifteen minutes or more of uncontrollable vomiting.

Both before and after this report by the Institute of Society, Ethics, and the Life Sciences, the Institute's Behavior Control Research Group surveyed the emerging applications of behavior-control technologies and found that particularly challenging problems and questions arose when the techniques in question were proposed for use within the setting of total institutions. Total institutions include prisons, juvenile detention facilities, rehabilitation centers, mental hospitals, and others. While behavior modifiers have applied their skills to some of the most difficult inmates in various prisons in an effort to turn them into obedient inmates and hopefully into obedient citizens, certain techniques were questioned at the conference.

Some programs have been compared to the popular

book and movie *A Clockwork Orange.* In it a violent offender is told that he can be released in a few weeks rather than serve his long prison sentence—providing he agrees to undergo a new treatment. After he consents, he is "cured" of his sexual problems and his aggressiveness through the use of aversive therapy.

Aversive therapy takes many forms. There is the simple type used on the obese who watched slides of rich food while receiving a mild shock. Or aversive therapy may involve the use of an instrument with such high voltage that it produces skin destruction. The punishment apparatus in the imaginary situation of *A Clockwork Orange* was so severe that the prisoner suffered vomiting just being strapped to the chair in which he was conditioned. His personality change was so complete that, when he returned to society, he was unable to function effectively. He was deprived of his behavior patterns of old—both good and bad—and, since he could no longer enjoy life, he attempted suicide.

In actual aversive therapy, only the unwanted behaviors are supposed to be erased. Behavior shapers and others who see benefits in behavior modification object to press stories that link treatment with such stories as *A Clockwork Orange.* Actually, some prisoners are eager to participate in behavior modification programs and it appears that many might benefit from well-designed programs. But the ethical implications of behavior control and the methods of administering programs need constant examining and further re-search.

START (a program for *S*pecial *T*reatment *A*nd *R*ehabilitative *T*raining) was a highly controversial behavior modification program with prisoners. It was in operation at the Medical Center for Federal Prisoners at Springfield, Missouri, from September 11, 1972, to March 1, 1974. It was developed to deal with offenders who had, in the authorities' view, failed to adjust satisfactorily to life in correctional institutions. This program for bending minds behind bars came under much attack.

Dr. Albert F. Scheckenbach, professional consultant for the program, described plans for it. He said that highly aggressive and assaultive individuals in the program

> will be confined to an isolated area until they have demonstrated consistently a potential to respond ap-propriately in normal institutional environments. Hence a unit has been developed that will provide for their needs . . . with movement to other areas of the institution prohibited except in dire emergencies.
>
> A status system is assigned as the initial treatment program for START. The status system involves a number of levels which differ as to their responsibili-ties and privileges and allows an inmate to work his way through different levels dependent on the appropriate-ness of his behavior. As an inmate consistently dem-onstrates his ability to get along at the current level to which he is assigned, he is rewarded by promotion to a

more privileged level. The progressive levels not only reward appropriate behavior but are also an incentive for the inmate to do better. The privileges have been reduced so that a high level of privileges can be attained only if the inmate is returned to population of a regular institution. The START program is based on the theory that appropriate behavior can be strengthened by reward and inappropriate behavior extinguished. Moreover, the use of the team approach in setting goals for each inmate allows for individual programming and increased flexibility of treatment within the rigid status system.

At the beginning of the program, inmates were placed in a solitary cell and allowed out of it only twice a week for showers and only once for exercise. If the prisoner behaved well for twenty days, he would be graduated to the next level, where his privileges would increase; for example, he would be allowed out of his cell for one and a half hours each day. Privileges were accorded on the basis of accumulated good days. However, since inmates' movement to higher levels depended on value judgments by individual guards, there were inequities. And since basic privileges were used as incentives, graduating to the highest level made life no more comfortable than in a typical federal prison. Abuses and the coercive nature of the program brought it to the attention of individuals concerned with human rights. The National Prison Project of the American Civil Liberties Union took the problems of some of the prisoners to court where there were adverse court rulings. While some of the cases were still pending, the Bureau of Prisons quietly canceled the program. In October 1975, Norman A. Carlson, the Federal Prisons Director, was quoted in *The New York Times* as saying that the program was phased out because it was too costly. He noted that START was called a behavior modification program; he believed if it had been called an "experiment in control" there would have been no problem.

A new prison at Butner, North Carolina, was originally referred to as the Center for Behavioral Research. It is now called the Federal Center for Correctional Research. The U.S. Congress Subcommittee on Constitutional Rights has been concerned about the use of mind control experiments that might be part of the programs to be developed and tested at Butner. It has received repeated assurances that no aversive conditioning of any kind will be used.

START is not the only program that has been halted. Much controversy and concern stemmed from the introduction of a number of behavior modification programs, since halted, in various prisons. In some cases, the prison authorities appear to have taken over the program started by the doctors and used it as a tool for maintaining order. One of the most notorious cases of mistreatment in the name of behavior therapy took place at Vacaville Rehabilitation Center in California. Prisoners there were placed in a labyrinth of cells where the only way out was through a series of stages determined by rewards for good behavior. Other prisoners were subjected to sensory deprivation in solid white rooms for long periods of time. The use of the drug apomorphine was halted at Iowa Security Medical Facility. Only if the inmate gives written consent can it be administered, and he can revoke this consent at any time. The court declared its use without voluntary consent to be cruel and unusual punishment.

The problem of informed consent has been the cause of controversy in these programs and in similar ones in a number of prisons. Where the goal of behavior modification is to give prisoners the behaviors they need to live in the outside world, it appears to have a positive effect on the life of the prisoner. If it is successful, society also benefits. Should prisoners who want help be denied the opportunity? This is a question some proponents are asking today.

In 1974, funding for programs supported by the Law Enforcement Assistance Administration were halted in an effort to stop abuses. Programs supported by other sources were allowed to continue unless stopped for other reasons. Whether programs are helpful or abusive seems to depend partly on whether they are administered as a means of control or punishment, or to give prisoners the opportunity to grow as individuals. For example, certain programs with child molesters and rapists have had a degree of success. These individuals tend to be very bad at sensing when they are being rejected or accepted; many falsely believe that their victims are leading them on. Through behavior therapy, they may learn to communicate with others so that they can recognize rejection.

Some new projects that involve "bending of minds behind bars" are a far cry from the programs formerly used for sexually disordered offenders. Poorly administered programs seem to add to the prisoner's humiliation and degradation. In helpful programs, behavior therapy is supportive of individual needs.

A prisoner who suffers from severe unprovoked violence may volunteer for psychosurgery. This involves the destruction or stimulation of parts of the brain through the use of surgery, radiation, or other techniques in an effort to alter the patient's behavior. Even where there is no known brain disease causing the problem, the destruction of extremely small parts of tissue in certain areas can modify behavior.

A frontal lobotomy is an operation on the frontal part of the brain. It results in a radical personality change. Between 1940 and the mid-1950s, according to medical records, about 50,000 such operations were performed throughout the United States. Generally the results were unfavorable, although some of the undesirable symptoms were eliminated. Some patients could leave mental institutions and lead better integrated lives; but for this one had to pay a large penalty: emotions were blunted and intellectual powers deteriorated. Since results were so mixed, and since the development of new drugs accomplished the same therapeutic goals without surgery, most responsible scientists now feel that the classical frontal lobotomy is a technique that should be abandoned. Unfortunately, not everyone agrees.

Comparatively small numbers of people suffer from violent attacks of rage. While the roots of violence are multiple and complex, some doctors believe that "an appreciable percentage of the relatively few individuals guilty of repeated violence are to be found in the 5 to 10 percent of the population whose brains do not function in a perfectly normal way."*

Another form of surgery has been used to eliminate dangerous behavior by patients who assault people when they have attacks of rage. It destroys tissues in extremely small areas of the limbic brain. While psychosurgery of this type has been performed extensively in the United States and in some other countries in recent years, it is still highly experimental. "Sedative neurosurgery" makes people quiet and manageable, but its dangers are undisputed.

On the other hand, there are individuals who want psychosurgery. What of the doctors who wish to help such people? One prisoner reportedly wrote to doctors all over the country in an effort to have psychosurgery performed on him. He had raped and killed two women and was sentenced to life imprisonment with

*Vernon Mark and Frank R. Ervin, *Violence and the Brain* (New York: Harper and Row, 1970), p. 5.

no possibility of parole. But he thought that if someone could operate on his brain, his attacks of violence
might be eliminated. Should he be deprived of psychosurgery? Consider the following case.

In 1972, Doctors Ernst Rodin and Jacques Gottlieb
of the Lafayette Clinic in Michigan filed a proposal
"For the Study of Treatment of Uncontrollable Aggression." The study was to include twenty-four criminal sexual psychopaths. The effect of surgery on a
portion of the limbic system of their brains would be
compared with the effect of a drug, cyproterone
acetate, on the male hormone flow. The comparison
was intended to show which, if either, could be used
in controlling aggression of males in prisons and to
afford lasting or permanent relief from such aggression to the patient.

However, only one suitable patient could be found
for the surgical procedure. This man, referred to as
John Doe, signed what was considered to be an
informed consent to undergo the surgery. The doctors
had also obtained consent from his parents for experimental techniques to be performed on his brain. Two
separate review committees of three people each were
established by Dr. Rodin to review the scientific
worthiness of the study and the validity of the consent.

John Doe had been charged with the murder and
rape of a student nurse at the Kalamazoo State
Hospital while confined there as a mental patient. He
had been committed to Ionia State Hospital in early

1955 as a criminal sexual psychopath. Under the terms of the then existing law, he had no trial for criminal charges. Many years later, he signed a consent for surgery stating that he understood a significant brain disturbance existed that might relate to his antisocial behavior. The consent included, among other things, permission for the investigators to destroy tissue in a very small portion of his brain if the problem appeared to be limited to a small area.

Early in 1973, the Detroit *Free Press* became aware of the work which the researchers were contemplating on John Doe, and court action was filed against them to prevent the surgery. There was considerable news-paper publicity; funds for the research project were stopped; and the case came to court.

In May 1973, John Doe was defended before a Michigan Circuit Court panel of three judges in what became a famous psychosurgery trial. It was brought to the attention of the panel that this man had been confined during more than half of his life at the Ionia State Hospital. Could he, in the light of this, give informed consent?

Dr. Peter Breggin, who was a witness at the trial, defined psychosurgery as the destruction of normal brain tissue for the control of emotions or behavior where abnormal tissue has not been shown to be the cause of the emotions or behavior in question. It is an indisputable fact that significant activity in the brain does not occur in isolation; it is correlated with activity in other parts of the brain. Therefore, it seemed certain that the understanding of the limbic system of the brain and its functions was very limited. And there could be no certainty of the results of the surgery.

Practically every witness at the trial helped to establish how little is known of the relationship of the limbic system to human behavior in the absence of some clearly defined clinical disease. Doctors Vernon Mark and Frank Ervin have noted repeatedly the primitive state of understanding of the amygdala, the part of the brain in question. They have expressed concern about the use of psychosurgery on individuals in state institutions; it would be too easy to use it to keep them quiet or to punish them. Dr. Mark, in a recent article in *Psychology Today,* remarks that psychosurgery outside of prisons can be an appropriate form of treatment. But under the present constraints of informed consent that exist in prisons, he does not think that it should be performed.

The testimony in the case of John Doe dramatized the need for extreme caution in any physical intervention in the brain. Brain surgery is considered irreversible in the sense that any intrusion into the brain destroys some brain cells and brains do not mend the way bones do.

It was unanimously agreed by all witnesses that, given the present state of the art, psychosurgery does not provide assurance that a dangerously violent person can be restored to the community. After long and involved testimony, the court found that the procedure was highly experimental and that institutional coercion meant that confined persons could not really consent freely to such a risky operation.

The controversy on the use of psychosurgery as a tool for mind control continued into 1976. Should this type of treatment be available for people who have attacks of uncontrollable violence and unprovoked aggression?

One such patient, known as Arthur P., was cited by Dr. Vernon Mark in a discussion at the Institute of Society, Ethics, and the Life Sciences. A twenty-nine-year-old ex-Marine, Arthur P. was an expert in both armed and unarmed combat. When a judge in county court confined him for repeated traffic violation, the prisoner went into his cell, smashed his hand through a brick wall, and ripped out the toilet bowl in one piece. On other occasions, he had injured people, put his hand through a wall, and so frightened doctors and nurses at a hospital that they refused to enter his room. Most episodes were in response to minor provocation and medication was no help. He was so dangerous that he could not be contained in either state hospitals or veterans' hospitals in the federal system. At the time of the report by Dr. Mark, after extensive study of the patient for over two and a half years, he was being considered for a hospital for the criminally insane. There he would be permanently isolated in a dungeon. At the time of the report, psychosurgery appeared to be the only solution.

Psychosurgery has political implications. Might psychosurgeons become thought controllers? Might some unscrupulous doctors bring undue pressures to operate on a patient or the patient's family? In one case, a thirty-four-year-old engineer, known as Thomas R., was subject to violent outbursts and did not respond to other treatments. He underwent a brain operation in which a small area deep inside his brain was deadened. This man did not have a single episode of rage for as long as four years after the operation. But a lawsuit was filed in his behalf charging that "the plaintiff was permanently injured and incapacitated, [and] has suffered great pain of body and mind."

The National Urban Coalition sponsored the first Minority Conference on Human Experimentation at Reston, Virginia, early in 1976. Here, the prevailing mood was against the use of psychosurgery unless it could be better regulated—this fact was highly emphasized. The speakers and the audience were, for the most part, members of minority groups and they agreed that minority groups had been consistently exploited in research.

Two black neurosurgeons presented papers on psychosurgery. Dr. Ernest A. Bates, of the University of California Medical Center at San Francisco, conceded that psychosurgery can at times relieve immense suffering and make a bad situation better; but he would consider it only as a last resort. Dr. Bates is opposed to the use of psychosurgery with prisoners, the mentally retarded, and children. Most participants in the conference agreed that existing controls were inconsistent and inadequate.

Many questions confronted the National Commission for the Protection of Human Subjects of Biomedical and Behavioral Research from the years 1974 to 1976. In September of 1976, the commission recommended that psychosurgery be permitted to continue on a research basis with strict safeguards for the rights and welfare of the patients. The commission concluded that the operations have potential merit when performed by competent neurosurgical teams. Among other recommendations, the commission specified that informed consent must be given, and patients must not feel coerced into joining any given research project.

Public debate continues—and so it should—about the use of mind control techniques both in and out of prisons. In a helpful report, Drs. Bertram Brown, Louis A. Wiencowski, and Stephanie B. Stolz brought together information on behavior modification and some of the critical issues surrounding it. Their report, issued by the National Institute of Mental Health, included fear of control. It stated:

> Although aversive therapy procedures seem more coercive than those using positive reinforcement, the individual still must cooperate fully with the procedures in order for them to be effective. While aversive procedures may reduce the individual's motivation to engage in the undesirable behavior, the motivation

probably will not be reduced to zero. Rather, the goal of the therapy generally is to reduce the motivation to the point where the individual is able to exercise self-control and avoid engaging in the undesirable behavior.

Recent fiction has dramatically portrayed individuals supposedly unable to overcome the effects of aversive therapy. This, however, is not realistic. If coercion is used in therapy—whether positive or aversive—that may indeed force the individual's cooperation for a time. But, in real life, once this coercion is removed, the individual will be able to return to his former ways if he is motivated to do so."*

Dr. Edward Marks, a Philadelphia clinical psychologist, notes in prisons, as everywhere, behavior is always being positively reinforced or met with aversive consequences. In an era when sexual and physical assault on prisoners by guards and other inmates still widely exists, and when theft, fear, intimidation, and even murder occur in almost all prisons, it seems rather foolish to question the morality of giving prisoners tokens or privileges for more socialized behavior. The problem is less with behavior modification techniques than with those who administer them. If an ethical scientist maintains the control, much good can be done. If the control reverts to untrained guards or corrupt prison administrators, then behavior modi-

*Bertram Brown, Louis A. Wiencowski, and Stephanie B. Stolz, "Behavior Modification: Perspective on a Current Issue," National Institute of Mental Health (Washington, D. C.).

fication just becomes another tool to maintain power and control over the prisoners.

Continued monitoring both by the public and by professional people is needed to balance risk against benefit and to build in safeguards against abuse for even the best-planned programs.

6 ALPHA WAVES, BIOFEEDBACK, AND OTHER APPROACHES

■ Are your friends "tuning in to alpha," meditating, talking about levels and altered states of consciousness? A flood of techniques claiming to teach self-mind control have come into being lately. They are a response to the need to relieve the stresses and strains of today's living. For millions of people, these techniques appear to accomplish their goals.

Many scientists and doctors agree that tensions today are greater than ever, and that relaxation techniques help people to cope with the added stress. Physicians estimate that from 50 percent to 75 percent of human disabilities are related to stress. This condition can be triggered by a variety of factors. Significant events in everyday life—a move to another city, a new teacher, a new brother or sister, a divorce, a vacation, illness of a family member—produce varying amounts of stress. Noise pollution and other intrusions in everyday affairs can also cause this condition. While different events have varying amounts of influence on body mechanisms, the more adjustments a person must cope with at any particular time, the more likely that s/he will suffer from a disease such as ulcers, or the type of high blood pressure apparently caused by stress.

Psychosomatic diseases, those influenced by the emotional state of a person, are particularly responsive to some of the new self-regulatory, or mind control, therapies. Other exciting aspects of self-mind control are the preventive and the pleasurable.

Small numbers of Yoga and Zen masters have known for hundreds of years how to control involuntary functions such as respiratory and heart rates. Recent scientific studies of ancient Yoga and meditation techniques combined with the development of feedback technology provide scientists with measures of actual changes in physiological states. Thousands of people who know little about what is really happening inside their bodies report that they feel better, have greater awareness and energy, and function more effectively in their work after the deep calm of meditation. But although each type of therapy or mind control has devoted followers who think their way is superior to others, some scientists point out that there is more than one way to meditate and many techniques are improving health through relaxation. Health professionals are increasingly exploring these techniques, but much is still not understood.

Many techniques deal with *alpha waves.* Alpha waves are the brain rhythm that accompanies certain relaxed states of feeling. If you close your eyes, relax your body, and think pleasant thoughts, your brain will probably generate frequencies that could be measured in a pattern of 8 to 13 cycles per second when recorded on an electroencephalograph. The existence of electrical impulses in the brain was known as long ago as 1875, but the electrical activity was not successfully recorded until the 1920s, when Hans Berger used an instrument that drew lines on paper. After a time the procedure of measuring the brain's electrical patterns became fairly common in hospital and research laboratories. The voltages of the brain are very small but many signals can be detected at once, for there is a constant storm of activity. The use of skilled technicians and computers has helped in interpreting these signals.

While no one considers the brain as a great source of electrical power, its activity can be correlated with various states of alertness of the normal person. One pattern of waves is most evident when a person is mentally active. This is *beta,* a pattern whose characteristic is 13 to 30 cycles per second on the electroencephalograph record. Alpha waves are the slower 8 to 13 cycles per second. Waves most prevalent in the stage of consciousness reached just before sleep are called *theta*: they are recorded at 4 to 8 cycles per second. *Delta* waves are produced during sleep or other forms of unconsciousness and have a frequency of 1 to 4 cycles per second.

Alpha waves mixed with beta waves are present in the records of about 90 percent of people when they close their eyes and sit quietly, thinking of nothing in particular. As one drifts toward sleepiness, theta frequencies begin to appear in the pattern, and there is less alpha and beta. Delta waves are not normally present except during deep sleep. Many relaxation techniques help people to increase the amount of alpha waves. Some aim to teach people to produce alpha waves with their eyes open and to be able to think in this state.

Students of Yoga and Zen produce unusually large amounts of alpha activity soon after they begin to meditate and show evidence of theta waves as their meditation continues. In addition, some masters of Eastern religions have shown the ability for voluntary control of processes considered by most Westerners to be completely involuntary. Through meditation and training in biofeedback a number of Westerners have been able to exercise control of certain body processes such as heart rate, respiration, and body temperature. But the significance of alpha waves and other brain waves is not completely understood even after careful examination with some of the best technology available.

Long before the refinement of biofeedback equipment in the Western world, Dr. Johannes H. Schultz developed a technique known as *autogenic training*. Around the year 1910, he helped patients in Germany to relax tense muscles and to control some of their so-called involuntary processes by having them silently repeat phrases such as "I am at peace," and "My right arm is heavy and relaxed." The development of modern techniques such as that described in G. D. Read's *Childbirth Without Fear* are based on principles of autogenic training. Dr. Herbert Benson in his recent, popular book, *The Relaxation Response*, describes autogenic training as evoking the same physiological changes as the relaxation response.

Dr. Schultz, a psychiatrist and neurologist, based his therapy on six exercises that were physically oriented and seven exercises that were primarily meditative. Later, special exercises for specific organs were added to his program. Exercises were done in a quiet room at comfortable temperature and under soft lighting conditions. As with other relaxation procedures, clothing was loose and comfortable, and the body posture could be a simple sitting position or reclining in a chair. In addition to this, autogenic training subjects could use the horizontal position, not recommended for some of the more modern relaxation techniques.

Autogenic training begins with the physical exercises. These are practiced for short periods at first, with an increase of time for each as one advances in the training. After the standard physical exercises are mastered in a period of about six to twelve months, the trainee is ready to start the meditative group. This training is long and time-consuming, and it may produce unpleasant side effects if practiced without the aid of a trained person. The goal, as with many other techniques, is to shift at will from a state of stress to one of relaxation.

Exercise 1 asks the trainee to imagine a feeling of heaviness in his/her arms and legs. Exercise 2 changes the focus of heaviness to an imagined sense of warmness in the limbs. In exercise 3, one imagines that s/he can control the rate of heartbeat by mind control. In exercise 4, there is concentration on breathing, and 5 calms by centering thoughts on the central portion of the body and repeating, "My solar plexus is warm." The sixth exercise concentrates on cultivating feelings of coolness in the forehead. All the exercises are to be done with passive concentration as opposed to active or intensive concentration.

As most Americans are in a hurry to obtain the benefits of relaxation responses, few approach it through the lengthy autogenic training in which meditative exercises must be practiced for months after mastering the standard exercises described above. Autogenic therapy has been much more popular in Europe. In the United States, Dr. Elmer E. Green, research psychologist at the Menninger Foundation, his wife, Alyce M. Green, and their colleague E. Dale Walters did some pioneering work combining autogenic training and biofeedback starting in 1966. In a research program with thirty-three women, they found that some were able to achieve self-regulation of a normally involuntarily controlled process—increasing the temperature on the fronts and backs of their hands. This supported the literature that certain physiological processes could be self-regulated. Combining some autogenic techniques with biofeedback highly accelerated the complicated process of voluntary control over "involuntary" processes.

The principles of biofeedback are simple. Living things have countless systems of feedback. For instance, information is fed back through the brain and nervous system directing action. When you reach for a pear on a table, your eyes tell your brain when your hand is close to the pear; then your muscles stop you from going beyond it or crashing into it. When you scratch an itch, you are also using biofeedback.

Learning of any sort depends on feedback. Your body has many internal feedback systems involving digestion, circulation, and so forth. On the whole, your body runs its thousands of individual systems with marvelous efficiency. Dr. Lewis Thomas, an eminent doctor and author, suggests that it is better to let the body run itself without mental interference. As he says in his book, *The Lives of a Cell*, "I am, to face facts squarely, considerably less intelligent than my liver."* Researcher Alyce Green agrees with Dr. Lewis

*Lewis Thomas, *The Lives of a Cell* (New York: Viking Press, 1974), p. 66.

in cases where the body is working well. But she notes that when it is not, biofeedback may help. Certainly, many people have been trained to restore health through proper control of mind and emotions. Many researchers feel that monitoring involuntary nervous functions such as heart and respiratory rates may prove valuable in controlling emotions and certain illnesses.

Experiments with body activities that are normally thought to be under automatic or nonconscious control were carried out by many investigators. In one study, heart rate, blood pressure, rate of intestinal contraction, and rate of formation in urine were changed in rats that were rewarded for their actions. Prof. Neal Miller of Rockefeller University, who ran the study, presented the results of these experiments at the International Congress for Psychology in London in the summer of 1969. He called for radical reorientation of thinking in connection with the actions of the glands and internal organs. Later, he worked on the principle of biofeedback with volunteers in a New York hospital. They learned to reduce blood pressure and slow down hearts that were beating too fast; however, a large number were not able to accomplish this to a degree that made it therapeutically useful. In one experiment, Miller and his colleagues were able to help some epileptic patients suppress the abnormal electric activity in their brains—a characteristic of their condition; but there is a considerable step between this and the control of seizures.

An outstanding pioneer in the field of biofeedback is Dr. Barbara Brown, author of *New Mind, New Body.* In this book, she describes extensive research in the world of biofeedback. There are studies that show the skin's ability to reveal the mind's unconscious reactions to reality, experiments in control of blood pressure, brain waves, heartbeat, muscles, mental activity, and altered states of consciousness.

Dr. Brown even shows how she taught people to use brain-wave feedback apparatus to run a toy train. When there were large amounts of alpha waves in the brains of the people, the voltage was extracted from the bursts to start the train running on its track. The voltage was amplified to increase power and filtered into an even flow before it was fed into the train. The larger the waves, the faster the train moved. And when alpha waves disappeared, the train stopped. This toy train technique is being used in many clinical studies of hyperactive children with marked success.

Biofeedback studies cover a wide range in medicine, education, and other fields with over two thousand scientific publications reporting positive results. Learning continues in this challenging and exciting field.

Suppose you are learning to control your blood pressure through biofeedback. As you lie relaxed on a couch in the laboratory, you are fitted with an instrument that measures your blood pressure. However, your blood pressure rises; a buzz indicates it, reporting a situation of which you are otherwise unaware. By trial and error you learn to quiet your thoughts and relax your tensions so that the buzzer in the machine does not sound. While visual or audible signaling devices help patients to learn to control blood pressure in the laboratory with the use of biofeedback, not enough research has been done to determine whether the results have lasting significance.

When biofeedback was first introduced, researchers were extremely hopeful that it would be a means of curing migraine headaches. Self-regulation of the autonomic nervous system appears to be successful in some cases of migraine, but researchers know that a certain number of ailments vanish simply because of positive thinking that they will ("placebo effect") rather than because of biofeedback. Dr. Miller believes that biofeedback does hold promise, but that much work needs to be done to evaluate it. In the migraine headache study at the Menninger Clinic, results give some indication of success with biofeedback. Of the patients who had suffered for years with severe migraines that were unrelieved by medication, 80 percent received some measure of relief. Some patients reported total relief for a period of several years. Other serious researchers claim similar results.

The knowledge that biofeedback can be used to monitor alpha waves produced by the brain led to a great variety of commercial biofeedback instruments. People seeking a kind of instant peace took lessons and bought equipment through magazine advertisements or from agents. Many people become involved in "getting high on alpha" at training centers and by the use of commercial alpha feedback machines. This kind of self-mind control may be fun, but scientists who are serious about biofeedback and the study of alpha waves know that inexpensive devices often feed back false information and have little value in dealing with illnesses. Those who spend the money for many popular courses and equipment may think that they will accomplish in minutes the kind of control of involuntary or autonomic nervous functions that Yoga and Zen masters have known for centuries. These masters spent long periods of time in accomplishing their techniques, and some have shown amazing control.

For example, Dr. Elmer Green's research with the Yogi Swami Rama and other people with unusual abilities of control has helped to develop a new blend of Eastern theory and Western technology. This has been referred to as a new "science of consciousness." After training in the Himalayas in the discipline of Yoga, Swami Rama came to the United States. At the Menninger Foundation in Topeka, Kansas, Dr. Green and his coworkers studied Swami Rama to examine the brain rhythms present during various shifting states of mind or levels of awareness. Dr. Green and his colleagues found him a cooperative subject for their Voluntary Controls Project 1970. The Yogi demonstrated that he could raise the temperature of the little-finger side of his right palm so that it differed from the thumb side by nine degrees Fahrenheit. One half of his palm turned pink; the other half turned gray. There was no noticeable motion of any muscles. Swami Rama explained that "all of the body is in the mind, but not all of the mind is in the body." This may seem confusing. In Yoga theory, the body is a field of energy that includes both body and mind. Yogis believe that all body processes are mind processes. Dr. Green and Alyce M. Green suggest that viewing body, mind, and spirit as structural expressions of one basic energy could help explain how some people can regulate their mind-body processes.

Unusual people such as Swami Rama show outstanding abilities in self-regulation. In addition to altering hand temperatures at will, Swami Rama has performed many other feats, such as voluntary control of his heart by causing it to cease pumping blood for seventeen seconds.

One of the other unusual people whom the Greens examined is Jack Schwarz, a Westerner who was born in Holland. Jack Schwarz was aware of his ability to control pain as a child even before he came to the United States. At the Menninger Clinic, he was wired to instruments that recorded his brain waves and other variables that give indication of stress, such as heartbeat, breathing rate, galvanic skin response, and skin temperature, while he pushed an unsterilized sailmaker's needle into his biceps. At the first attempt, his arm bled somewhat, but it stopped about one second after he said it would. On the second attempt, which followed immediately, there was no bleeding.

Jack Schwarz explained that in cases of voluntary control of bleeding and pain, he thinks of his arm as an object rather than a part of his body that is attached to him. "Detachment" is a well-known Yoga method for control of pain, and it is associated with the increased production of alpha waves. There are records of Indian Yogis who continued in the "alpha state" when touched with hot glass test tubes. Detachment such as this cannot be accomplished by a few simple lectures in a mind control course, although some courses advertise such claims.

Dr. Green feels that the importance of this type of demonstration was not to show that people such as Jack Schwarz and Swami Rama can do unusual things, but to show that conscious control (self-regulation) of a number of "involuntary" processes can be learned. Dr. Green is especially interested in the relationship of voluntary control of physiological processes in connection with the establishment and maintenance of psychosomatic health. He says, if every young student *"knew* by the time he finished his first biology class, in grade school, that the body responds to self-generated psychological inputs, that blood flow and heart behavior, as well as a host of other body processes, can be influenced at will, it would change prevailing ideas about both physical and mental health. It would then be quite clear and understandable that we are individually responsible to a large extent for our state of health or disease.

"Perhaps then people would begin to realize that it is not life that kills us, but rather it is our reaction to it, and this reaction can be to a significant extent self-chosen."*

*Elmer E. Green, Alyce M. Green, and E. Dale Walters, *A Demonstration of Voluntary Control of Bleeding and Pain*, Research Dept., Menninger Foundation (Topeka, Kansas, 1972).

7 HYPNOSIS AND COMMERCIAL MIND CONTROL COURSES

■ Hypnosis is a form of mind control that has been studied for over two hundred years and practiced for several thousand years. It was used by priests in Egypt and Greece in "sleep temples" hundreds of years before Christ. Today, it is gaining in popularity as a form of mind control that helps a long list of problems. But what exactly is hypnosis?

How you define hypnosis depends on how you view it. Opinions vary greatly. Certainly, it is a form of mind control and an altered state of consciousness. It could be described as a state of heightened suggestibility induced by another person or by oneself, usually induced by bodily relaxation and concentration on a narrow range of stimuli.

Medical hypnotism was first developed in Europe by

Franz Mesmer, a late eighteenth-century Austrian physician who was interested in mysticism. He cured many psychosomatic ailments by suggestion or hypnosis, which he called "animal magnetism." In 1841, a Scottish surgeon, Dr. James Braid, attended some exhibitions of mesmerism, the phenomenon discovered by Mesmer. Dr. Braid recognized that it was not animal magnetism that caused the trancelike state; instead he described it as a suspension of the conscious mind, forced into weariness through repetitive stimuli. He coined the word *hypnotism*, but , in honor of Mesmer, mesmerism is still an accepted synonym.

Some authorities claim that there is no such thing as hypnosis since there is no scientific way to tell whether a person is hypnotized. No one has developed a test that establishes this condition by the examination of brain waves, pulse rate, skin response, eye movements, or any other means. But although there is no scientific way to tell whether a person is hypnotized, there are some common criteria. These include "inability" to open eyes, the kind of thinking in which words are taken literally, the seeming weight change in arms and legs, and, under deep hypnosis, anesthesia. Partial amnesia, hallucinations, and a certain muscular rigidity may also be symptoms. But people argue about the criteria. Martin Orne, Ph.D. and M.D., disputes these criteria. In his view, the subject learns to do under hypnosis what s/he thinks is *expected*; therefore, the effects could be produced without hypnosis. Those who use hypnosis claim that about 90 percent of the youth in any population can be hypnotized to some degree. Nearly 70 percent of all adults are susceptible to hypnosis if they wish to cooperate.

While theories on hypnosis vary, methods of producing a trance are familiar to many people. A subject is persuaded to relax and fix his/her attention on the hypnotist's directions while the hypnotist repeats certain phrases or sentences, along with suggestions and encouragement.

Although inducing a trance may not be difficult, bringing the person back to the normal self may be, if the individual happens to be emotionally unstable or if the correct procedure is not used. Suppose that a man has been put into a trance and told that he cannot open his eyes, lift his arms, or move his legs. He may even be told that his body is stiff, and that he can lie between two chairs supported only by his head and feet. This is a popular stage procedure. Now the hypnotist tells the man that he will say the letters from A to F and that at A he will sit up in his chair, at B he will be able to move his legs freely, at C he will move his arms, and so on. Finally, the man is told that he will feel the way he did before being hypnotized. After the plan is given under hypnosis, it is put into action.

Stage hypnotists entertain at the expense of their subjects, most of whom volunteer for the experience. For the great majority of people, it is a harmless experience. But there is danger in some cases that the person will suffer from further emotional upset. The hypnotist should be a qualified person who has trained by taking courses and passing examinations. Most qualified hypnotists oppose the use of hypnosis for entertainment. A qualified hypnotist can be found listed in the Directory of the American Society of Clinical Hypnosis.*

In the opinion of some psychologists and psychiatrists who have taken commercial mind control courses, the courses are a form of hypnotic programming. Those who offer the courses claim that this is not the case. However, if it is, one should consider the fact that the teachers are not qualified hypnotists. Some professionals in the field of mind control are concerned about what misinformation and false hopes are doing to some of the hundreds of thousands of people who are being instructed. According to Victoria Y. Pellegrino, a person who took the four-day Silva Mind Control Course and wrote about it in *Today's Health*, November, 1975, published by the American Medical Association, the training of the instructors lasts for two weeks. Following this, there is a year of supervision while they teach. In addition to their share in the profit from the tuition paid by those who take the course, instructors make a profit from the books and products they sell. One of these products is an experimental "Cheops Pyramid Tent," selling for $30; it has

---

*The Society is located at 2400 E. Devon Avenue, Suite 218, Des Plaines, Illinois 60018.

an accompanying brochure that states, "People using the Pyramid Tent claim they are surrounded with energy."

Mind control courses make many claims about increasing a person's energy and abilities. In a demonstration lecture, you may be told that the course will teach you to relax, control pain, improve your skills, develop your psychic abilities, correct disturbing bad habits, effect changes in your personality. The instructor may admit that some of the promises sound unreal, but add that he, too, was a skeptic when first introduced to the method of mind control he now teaches. When he was a salesman, he suffered from allergies, which have disappeared now that he uses mind control to "tap a part of his mind that was not available to him before."

The speaker at the demonstration lecture suggests that you can tune in your mind to make greater use of your intelligence. He claims Albert Einstein and Thomas Alva Edison used their alpha waves when they were inventing many things and solving difficult problems. By taking this course, the speaker implies, you can use your mind the way they did. If not, your money will be refunded.

During the four days of the course, students are exposed to conditioning processes to help reach the "alpha level." Basically, conditioning involves being in a relaxed position, breathing deeply, and listening to a tape player that produces a repetitious sound much like the clack of a metal wheel. Along with this, the instructor's soothing and confident voice tells you that you are now able to use more of your mind and use it in a special manner. You are increasing your mental facilities for serving humanity in a better way. S/he even repeats the old familiar, "Every day in every way, I am getting better and better." People who take the course say their minds drift during these exercises; some doctors believe they are hypnotized, despite the disclaimers of those who offer the course. The instructor brings students back to their everyday level by telling them they will awaken feeling better than ever before, and so they do.

Directions given during the conditioning exercises vary somewhat from one instructor to another, but they all sound much like the techniques used by hypnotists. The clicking sound on the tape player is similar to the noise of a metronome, and may be the recording of one. This instrument was used by Mesmer in his experiments in hypnotism. The teacher uses a tone of voice similar to one hypnotists use. The verbal instructions include directions for keeping your eyes fixed on a point in the ceiling: "Stare at it, keep staring. Feel your lids grow heavy. Feel your eyes wanting to close as the lids grow heavy. Keep your eyes open until they close all by themselves."

Dr. Elmer Green, in a letter to the editor of the *National Observer* several years ago, wrote that it is probably useful for people to relax during the exercises described above; however, he feels it should be made clear that the results obtained depend more on hypnosis than on changes in brain-wave patterns. He points out that many scientific objections might be removed if mind control teachers made it clear that they are training a state of consciousness, and that alpha waves may or may not be present.

Part of mind control training in the Silva Method is devoted to developing powers of ESP (extrasensory perception). Students press small cubes of stainless steel, copper, bronze or lead to their foreheads, "descend into alpha," and project themselves into the metals. They imagine themselves inside plants, animals, and the human anatomy. Although each student has signed a release in which s/he accepts the fact that mind control does not practice medicine, they "work cases." During part of the course, an instructor or a classmate gives another classmate the name, age, and address of a person unknown to them, projects an image of that person onto the wall of the imaginary lab which s/he has constructed earlier in the course, diagnoses the case, and invents a "cure." To assist themselves, students also invent a pair of "counselors"—one female and one male. Suppose one receives the name of a person who is suffering from arthritis. Suppose when this person, someone unknown to the student, is projected on the student's wall or imaginary screen, the hip bones are prominent. The student then "sends help and anoints her bones." The applied ESP part of the Silva Mind

Control course involves the working of existing problem cases through subjective communication and "mental projection for detection and correction of abnormalities at a distance."

While many graduates sing the praises of the Silva Mind Control and relatively few ask for a refund of the $175 tuition, some confess to feeling that it was an expensive way to learn how to relax and think positively. Some object to half-truths that creep into the instructors' lectures and to gimmicks used. One of these is the three-finger technique, which is claimed to bring about positive events through the power of your mind at alpha. With thumb, index finger, and middle finger of one hand held together as you envision something you want, what you seek should appear—for example, that parking place that is so hard to find on a crowded street. Thinking positively may help you to persevere, but no one explains how the three-finger technique puts you at alpha where you are "able to project your thoughts."

Dr. Green is concerned because mind control teachers are dealing with the unconscious; this can be dangerous in the hands of people who are not experts. Hypnotic programming into "psychic dimensions" may not be appropriate to a person's needs. What is correct for one person may be disastrous for another. Working with the human psyche is a delicate task and requires training and the availability of further help and counseling, should it be needed.

Dr. Lewis R. Wolberg is one of a number of

psychoanalysts pioneering in the medical use of hypnosis; or *hypnotherapy*. This involves the use of hypnosis combined with psychological treatment to relieve symptoms and to help in an understanding of the reasons for them. In his book *Hypnosis,* Dr. Wolberg points out that many symptoms such as ulcers, asthma, migraine, insomnia, arthritic pain, obesity, and depression can be symptoms of underlying disturbances. He stresses the need for trained and competent people as hypnotists, especially in the case of mental disturbances or disorders. Extreme anxiety after hypnosis may continue for several months in some subjects, and a well-meaning person might create considerable conflict in sensitive people. Well-trained doctors, on the other hand, can cope with such a situation to prevent personal harm. They may even be able to use posthypnotic reactions to advantage in a treatment process.

The American Medical Association approves the use of hypnosis by properly trained hypnotists in major operations to induce the kind of deep trance that such an operation requires. While open-heart surgery with hypnosis as the only anesthesia is unusual today, thousands of such operations were performed by English surgeons in India before chemical anesthesia was common. Further experimentation with hypnosis as general anesthesia was largely abandoned after ether was discovered as an anesthetic in the nineteenth century. But many dentists and doctors still use hypnosis on people whose physical conditions cannot stand the use of chemical anesthetics.

Applications of hypnosis to a variety of problems such as weight control, phobias, psychosomatic difficulties, breaking the smoking habit, and fear of flying are common today.

Some doctors find hypnosis a valuable asset in the practice of obstetrics to bring about relaxation during normal labor and delivery. Dr. Lynn A. Phelps, of the University of Wisconsin Medical School in Madison, is one of these. He teaches groups of four or five pregnant women for six hour-long sessions to hypnotize themselves at will. This knowledge of self-hypnosis may help them to relax during labor. It has the extra advantage of being able to provide analgesia, time distortion, and dissociation even if their babies should be born when their own doctors cannot be reached.

Imagine a woman in a dentist's chair preparing for some oral surgery on her gums. She has been trained to relax by self-hypnosis through a program at her local health center. She puts her right hand on her face and counts slowly to three. Her eyelids droop slowly until they are closed and the rigidity of her facial muscles lessens. Although she appears to be asleep, she answers the dentist when he asks if she is ready to begin the operation. When he cuts into the tissue, his patient remains calm and shows no sign of pain. He asks her to open her jaws more widely, and she obeys. Her self-hypnosis has enabled her to relax and feel no pain during what would normally be a very painful experience without tissue-numbing drugs.

Suggestibility plays an important part in hypnosis. The hypnotic trance state renders the mind more receptive to the hypnotist's suggestions. This is true whether the hypnotist is oneself or another person. People often wonder whether one can be made to do something immoral after being hypnotized, through the use of posthypnotic suggestion. Can a criminal hypnotist play "Big Brother" and during a trance persuade you to harm another person at a later time? Will you do his/her bidding during hypnosis if the act is something you would not do in your usual state of consciousness?

Dr. Jacob H. Conn of the Johns Hopkins School of Medicine is reported to have read through 150 years of case histories of hypnotism and to have found no proof of a violent crime committed under hypnosis. Still, the popular belief seems to be otherwise. Perhaps the people involved in those case studies were never exposed to suggestions of violence by the hypnotist. Or might violent cases not have been reported?

Charles Manson, famous for the Sharon Tate murder of 1969, was accused of hypnotizing and thus leading his followers long after he was jailed, through posthypnosis. Sirhan Sirhan is described by Charles McQuiston, reportedly a United States intelligence officer, as having been hypnotically programmed to kill Robert Kennedy. McQuiston called Sirhan Sirhan a real-life "Manchurian candidate," after the character in the book of the same name. In it, conspirators program a man to assassinate a presidential candidate. There are claims that Sirhan Sirhan was brainwashed under hypnosis, that he heard constant repetition of ideas that made him feel worthless, then an idea of killing Robert Kennedy was implanted in his mind. This has never been confirmed.

The fact remains that *most* people will not carry out antisocial acts suggested when they are hypnotized. Dr. Milton Erickson, an Arizona psychiatrist who is considered an expert in the field of hypnosis, used various techniques in an effort to get people to perform antisocial acts while under hypnosis or after it. He failed consistently. In one case, a young man was asked to read his roommate's mail while under hypnosis. At first, he fumbled with the envelope, but he managed to remove the letter. Then he held it upside down. When this was corrected by the hypnotist, the young man found the writing illegible. When Dr. Erikson pointed out the words to him, the young man went temporarily blind (a condition that was relieved by the hypnotist).

However, in one case where a hypnotist was testing antisocial reactions, a woman did obey instructions to throw acid at him, but she immediately covered her face in horror. The hypnotist was behind a sheet of invisible glass, just in case. Subjects have been persuaded to take money from the pockets of overcoats belonging to other people, but in each case the hypnotist convinced the subject that the coat belonged to him/her.

In spite of these apparent contradictions, most authorities on hypnotism believe subjects do not lose the power to discriminate between right and wrong during hypnosis. A person who commits a crime after hypnosis would do so in any case. The only instances of antisocial acts by people who have been hypnotized are where awareness of the actual situation has been altered by means of illusion, amnesia, or hallucination. A person with great faith in a hypnotist might be persuaded to drink a liquid that contained poison, but a qualified hypnotist is no more likely to poison a person by such a trick than a qualified surgeon is likely to cut out a person's heart while the patient is under anesthesia. But what about an "unqualified" hypnotist? Almost everyone can learn to hypnotize.

Will hypnotism cause a person to have a weakened will or capacity to resist propaganda? Reports of people who stay in a trance after hypnotism and thus remain subject to suggestion indicate that the hypnotist was poorly trained or that the person suffered from underlying problems, or both. There are dangerous aspects to hypnosis. Putting someone in a trance is not for the amateur.

WHAT IS BRAINWASHING?

■ A political prisoner has been in a cell for a month in total isolation. There is no heat, no bed, and little food. A light burns day and night. He has tried to resist emotional confusion by reliving in his mind each moment of his life that he can remember, from early childhood to the present. He has resisted earlier efforts of indoctrination to new ideas in spite of a systematic approach to what is commonly called brainwashing. Now he lies on the cold floor, slipping in and out of consciousness. He sees a mouse coming through one of the tiny holes in the wall of his cell. Time and time again he tries to catch it for food, his mouth salivating at the thought of such a delicacy. But he can do no more than lie on the floor, shivering in the cold, covered only by filth. He reaches out toward the mouse, but it slips through his hands and he has no energy to chase it. After a time, he realizes that there is really no mouse coming into the cell through the walls, nor are there any holes through which it might come. He knows that this torture is only a part of the brainwashing technique that he is trying to resist.

Dr. Joost A. M. Meerloo has studied extensively the methods that captors use to bring "truth" to their victims' minds. In his famous book, *The Rape of the Mind*, Dr. Meerloo describes the tools used both in time of war and time of peace to accomplish mass submission. In his view, any person can be turned into a traitor by pressure on the weak points of his/her makeup.

The word "brainwashing" comes from the Chinese colloquialism *hsi nao*, which literally means "to wash the brain." In Robert Jay Lifton's authoritative book, *Thought Reform and the Psychology of Totalism: A Study of Brainwashing in China*, he suggests that one can apply to brainwashing the old Zen Buddhist maxim: "The more we talk about it, the less we understand it." Definitions vary, but there is general agreement that brainwashing is a powerful effort to manipulate the human mind.

According to a recent edition of the *Encyclopedia Britannica*, brainwashing consists of "various systematic efforts to persuade non-believers to accept a certain allegiance." It is described as a technique that has the same basic approach when it is used in a prison, a factory, a revolutionary college, or elsewhere. *The Encylopedia of Human Behavior,* edited by Robert M. Goldenson, defines brainwashing as "intensive propaganda techniques applied under conditions of stress." Conditions that undermine morale are used to pave the way for indoctrination with a set of beliefs that may produce a change in behavior.

The *Random House Dictionary of the English Language* defines brainwashing first as "a method for systematically changing attitudes or altering beliefs originated in totalitarian countries, especially through the use of torture, drugs, or psychological-stress techniques." A second definition includes "any method of controlled systematic indoctrination, especially one based on repetition and confusion: brainwashing by TV commercials."

Do you think you have been brainwashed by advertising on television? Feminists claim that girls are brainwashed into passive roles. To what extent can you be coerced without your consent or knowledge? Was Patricia Hearst brainwashed by her parents into becoming a loyal upper-class woman and then brainwashed again by the Symbionese Liberation Army into a hard-talking, gun-toting revolutionary? Some government officials feel that they were brainwashed into supporting the war in Vietnam by the military leaders of the United States.

Not only is it impossible to define the form of mind control known as brainwashing to everyone's satisfaction, it is impossible to understand what happens to a person in the process. Most people agree that the process involves several factors, all operating more or less at the same time. Four phases seem to be involved, generally in the following order, although they may overlap: emotional assault, calculated kindness and leniency, confession, and reeducation.

In order for brainwashing to work on, for example, a prisoner of war, certain conditions must be present. First, s/he must be in a position where it is necessary to make a choice between cooperating or starving, being tortured or not, or even being allowed to live or being killed. In order to preserve one's physical existence, it may be necessary to give up loyalty, identity, and other values that the person normally holds very important. If the victim continues to resist after first attempts to produce cooperation, living conditions may be made even harsher. Or, on the other hand, if the person cooperates, rewards such as extra food may be provided.

Part of the process includes asking the subject to indulge in self-criticism if cooperation is achieved. Cooperation produces guilt feelings in the great majority of people. The use of harsh treatment alternated with friendly treatment helps to put the victim in a state of confusion. Worn out by physical mistreatment and emotional confusion, the person is in a state where thoughts can usually be indoctrinated with little resistance.

Another aspect of brainwashing technique is the use

of isolation. When leaders and friends are removed, certain personality changes take place even in those people who normally enjoy being alone. The absence of friends and leaders who normally supply emotional support make it more difficult to resist indoctrination. The individual becomes more vulnerable to threats and bribes. Experiments with people in isolation in many scientific laboratories confirm this. For example, at the University of Manitoba, in Winnipeg, Canada, subjects reported hearing birds chirping and waves splashing on the shore after two weeks of isolation far from any sounds of nature. Auditory and visual illusions are commonly reported after experiments in sensory deprivation. An interesting aspect of the Canadian experiment was that the volunteers emerged from isolation with an attitude of noncaring toward everything. This attitude lasted for three to eight days, depending on the subject.

During isolation experiments, changes in brain waves have been noted. Verbal, mathematical, and perceptual abilities are impaired after a week of confinement. Even shorter periods of isolation have been known to cause the imagination to run wild. In some cases, the nerve endings in the skin send messages that small animals are crawling over the skin even though none are present. Certainly, isolation can have severe effects on the whole person. The human body may be better able to cope with such things as city traffic, wild animals, and hurricanes.

Experiments at the University of Michigan's Mental

Health Research Institute showed that men and women responded in much the same way to sensory deprivation. The instructions given before the isolation experiences seemed to play a part in the bizarre hallucinations that sometimes occurred during the experiments, and it seemed possible to increase the amount of anxiety by suggestion.

In actual practice, a combination of factors, including isolation and fostering attitudes of suspicion and distrust, is developed to make the conditioning process of thought control more easily accepted.

From ancient times to the present, various groups of people have used the techniques of confession and reeducation to change attitudes and beliefs of others. Are these merely gentler forms of brainwashing? Picture a primitive tribe holding a meeting in which emotions are aroused by drumming in a rhythmic manner and by dancing for long periods of time. Excitement reaches a peak when some of the members perform solo dances to the accompaniment of hand clapping by the group. This clapping continues for many minutes, or even hours, in a strong rhythm. Here and there a person goes into a trance or collapses with fatigue. Suggestibility is very high and the message that the leaders wish to convey is repeated again and again. The group sings along in submission and gratitude for the experience of conversion. Patterns of thought and behavior can be established in this way, and those which have already been implanted can be reinforced.

Whether you call this type of experience a form of brainwashing or not depends on semantics. If you define brainwashing only in the political sense, it does not apply. But if you include all changes in behavior by confession and reeducation, many religious experiences may fall under the broad definition. In this case, you may feel that not all brainwashing is bad.

The results of brainwashing may be considered good or bad depending on one's personal beliefs. A person who believes s/he is possessed by the devil may find relief in a voodoo ceremony that in the broad sense "washes the brain and cleanses it" of evil spirits. Both the individual and his/her loved ones see the benefit in this.

Voodoo is an example of a most unwelcome form of mind control, especially in certain cases. Healthy people have become sick or even died after exposure to events that affect their minds with a sense of fear and/or guilt. In one tribe a man may be "boned" by having a bone pointed at him in a certain way by an enemy. Picture him staring at the bone. He lifts his hands as if to stop the terrible poison that he imagines flowing through his body. His face pales and his eyes become glassy. Now his body begins to tremble and even though he tries to scream, no sound comes from his mouth. After a short time, he falls down and moans as if suffering terrible pain. Then he becomes quiet, retreats to his bed, refuses to eat, and awaits death or a medicine man who can cast a counter-charm on him.

Many reports cite examples of people who have died after eating a kind of food that was considered taboo in their culture. Usually the victim does not know s/he is ingesting a forbidden food and finds out the true nature of the food after it has been eaten. The food may be harmless for most people, but for someone who believes it to be poison, the food may be the cause of death. This is difficult to understand, but it has been well documented by physiologists. It has been suggested that in a society where there is strong belief in the supernatural world, one who transgresses food customs or is subjected to a curse by an enemy may suffer from a kind of "surgical shock." According to this theory, a feeling of helplessness is reinforced by other members of the society, who treat the person as if s/he were already dead. The victim feels hopeless, and autosuggestion of the strongest kind becomes involved. According to theory, adrenaline is secreted in abnormal amounts over a long period of time, impairing the walls of the capillaries and allowing fluid to pass to the surrounding tissues. The volume of circulating blood thus is reduced. The result is a state of shock that leads to the deterioration of the nerve centers and the heart, and eventually to death.

This theory has not been proven, but it is known that the power of mind control can bring about death.

In many countries, various approaches to religious conversion to Christiantity are based on fear and guilt. People may be threatened with the certainty that hell awaits unsaved sinners. Strong emotions are excited in an effort to disrupt old thought patterns and introduce or maintain the law of the gospel. To many families, this seems a good thing. But when conversion to a form of religion separates children or young adults from their families, the leaders of the religious sect are often accused of brainwashing. Further information about this form of mind control is discussed in the next chapter.

Many psychologists and psychiatrists have been accused of brainwashing in their use of behavior modification, and some have been accused of it in their use of psychotherapy. Opponents admit that patients have a variety of countercontrol measures available to them that effectively preclude any unwanted influence of a controller or therapist. Professor G. Terence Wilson, a Rutgers University authority on behavioral conditioning techniques, believes that those who suggest conditioning is brainwashing on a mass basis simply miss the point of behavior therapy. Aversive conditioning needs the cooperation of the patient or client. For example, in the case of behavior therapy for alcoholics, the therapist is acting as problem solver and uses a personalized approach for each client. The latter must trust and respect the therapist. This is far different from the brainwashing concept, in which subtle changes in attitudes are brought about without an individual's awareness that changes are being made.

Another part of the controversy concerns itself with whether or not brainwashing or behavioral conditioning techniques can be used to dramatically change the way a person or group of people behaves. Here, again, the way brainwashing is being defined is crucial.

Many psychologists believe that all individuals have their breaking points, but that a strong sense of self or identity can help brainwashing victims, such as political prisoners, to maintain their integrity and dignity for a longer period of time. Some prisoners of war have been able to find meaning and value even under the stress of incredible suffering. *

Was Patty Hearst brainwashed? This question was in the fore when she was on trial in 1976 for participating in the burglary of the Hibernia Bank in California. Several psychiatrists who examined her for the defense believed she was brainwashed after her kidnapping on February 4, 1974, by members of the self-styled Symbionese Liberation Army. Dr. Lewis Jolyan West, chief of psychiatry at the University of California at Los Angeles, described her situation as a "classic case of coercive persuasion." Dr. West compared the treatment to which she was subjected to that of the American pilots captured during the Korean war. The pilots became propaganda vehicles for their Chinese and North Korean captors. Dr. West claimed that Patricia Hearst had to accept what the Symbionese Liberation Army told her to do or be killed. Her cooperation was a response to her fear of death.

Another psychiatrist who testified for the defense was Dr. Martin P. Orne, a University of Pennsylvania psychiatrist who specializes in simulation, or whether or not one was playing a role. He reported that he believed she was the victim of mistreatment and deprivation that made it possible for her captives to manipulate her mind.

The third psychiatrist for the defense was Dr. Robert Jay Lifton, professor of psychiatry at Yale University, an eminent authority on coercive persuasion. Dr. Lifton said that the SLA soldiers had broken Patricia Hearst's sense of identity and self by manipulating her mind. Her confessions were typical of mind-control victims.

Witnesses for the prosecution claimed that Ms. Hearst was not brainwashed but that she was living a lie. Dr. Harry Kozol, a well-known psychiatrist, testified that Ms. Hearst was a rebel without a cause who found her calling in terrorism. He described the heiress as an angry young woman "ripe for plucking" by terrorists whose beliefs echoed her own frustrated yearnings.

The subject of brainwashing, coercion, or thought control was of extreme importance for the defense in this case. If the value orientation was brought about by force through fear of death, so that the victim was brainwashed, she had no control over the behavior that followed the conversion. Dr. William Sargant, Britain's foremost expert on brainwashing, published in the mass media his five interviews with Ms. Hearst in the fall before the trial. According to him, she had undergone a forced conversion and was kept in control by the constant threat of death by either the SLA or the FBI. Dr. Sargant felt that a partial reconversion began when she was a fugitive in New York State with William and Emily Harris, but she still feared surrendering to the FBI. At this point, she may have been continually conditioned by the presence of the Harrises.

Dr. Sargant defended Ms. Hearst with the statement that he believed the last war showed that thirty days was the maximum period of tension and stress that a normal person could endure before breakdown. Many Americans feel that one should retain personal values no matter what the conditions are. They cite examples of prisoners of war who suffered great stress, both physical and mental, without breaking down to the will of their captors.

After release from captivity, when a person finds himself/herself in new circumstances where the imposed values are no longer rewarded, the effects of brainwashing usually fade away.

In the legal sense, the important question is whether the subject is really free to walk away from the captors, even though there is no physical restraint. Is the person acting voluntarily or because of the pressure that has forced a change of values? This is a factor in many conversions of cults mentioned in the next chapter of this book.

After a thirty-nine-day trial, the jury found Patricia Hearst guilty of taking part in the robbery at the Hibernia Bank. Her attorney, F. Lee Bailey, had attempted to prove that she had been brainwashed. He argued that she should be compared with prisoners of war, and pardoned. In his charge to the jury, Judge Oliver J. Carter noted that even though no one can directly examine a person's thoughts, the jury was entitled to infer intent from conduct. He is quoted as saying, "You are free to accept or reject the defendant's account of her experience with her captors. Duress or coercion may provide a legal excuse for the crime charged against her, but a compulsion must be present and immediate . . . a well-founded fear of death or bodily injury with no possible escape from the compulsion."

The comparison with other examples of brainwashing may in fact have weakened Ms. Hearst's case. In most brainwashing cases, the effects were relatively short. Patricia Hearst spent about ten weeks with the SLA before the bank robbery, and she was on the road with part of the group for about sixteen months after it. While the defendant's credibility and other factors entered into this famous case, one thing is certain. The jury did not accept brainwashing as an excuse for her actions.

Brainwashing, or whatever we call the process that involves shifts of attitudes through the use of confusion, emotional assault, deprivation, confession, and reeducation, varies in degree. A person's vulnerability to overpowering influence varies greatly indeed, and in the case of life-and-death situations, each case is different. More gentle persuasion, as in the case of advertising and religious conversions to modern cults (and in some cases to more established religions), appears to depend to a greater degree on predisposition to change one's opinion. It also depends on the kind and degree of exposure to persuasion. Such variation makes the word "brainwashing" even more difficult to establish and define.

9 MIND CONTROL AND THE RELIGIOUS CULTS

■ Who controls the minds of the converts to the thousands of currently popular religious cults such as Sun Myung Moon's Unification Church, the Children of God, and Hare Krishna? Are their recruiting procedures a form of brainwashing or are these cults simply a haven for people who desire a life with less emphasis on the materialistic world? What is happening in these different sects whose members seem far removed from the world in which they once lived? Are young people being exploited by wealthy leaders through peer pressure and mind control?

Many people have tried to rescue their children or young adult sons and daughters from various cults, often without success. One nineteen-year-old girl who was selling candy for the Unification Church at a

Connecticut shopping center was abducted by friends of her parents who wanted to return her to her home in Vermont. They hoped to undo what they considered brainwashing and help her return to her previous life-style, which they considered normal. Since the girl was not a minor, the attempted "rescue" failed; she was free to return to the community of the Unification Church, where she was a devout member of the family.

With a reported membership of 2 million worldwide, Moon's Unification Church is claiming much attention. The church's doctrine is quite different from the religious beliefs most of the American members held when they were growing into adolescence. Some outsiders think of it as a combination of anti-Communist psychology, Pentecostal Christianity, Eastern mysticism, and metaphysics. According to Moon, God intended Adam and Eve to marry and have perfect children. This would have established the kingdom of heaven on earth. But Satan, in the form of a snake, seduced Eve and spoiled the plan. Jesus was sent to redeem the world, but He, too, failed to fulfill God's plan. The Reverend Moon believes he was called to be a prophet and to bring the world the message of truth that would prepare it for the return of Christ. Some say he thinks of himself as a second Messiah, although he stops short of proclaiming himself in this role. Moon preaches of fire and hell in a highly charged manner in his native tongue. Emotions are intense. For some, he appears to produce a drugless high.

Although the Moonies, as the followers are called, are forbidden to use drugs, many observers have remarked on the glassy, spaced-out look in their eyes. Like the girl in the Connecticut shopping center, the Moonies sell their candy to raise funds with a smile that appears everlasting. Lack of sleep has been suggested as a reason for their glassy eyes. But glassy eyes may also be related to a trancelike state or hysteria produced by the assault on the emotions of a fiery conversion process.

Why would anyone work long hours, live an austere life, and believe a doctrine so different from earlier teachings? Psychologists have compared the cult to a warm womb for adolescents who want to return to a safer period of life. In their search for identity, adolescents may feel intoxicated with a sense of growth and freedom, but they may also feel a considerable amount of loneliness and fear. Is the Unification Church a refuge for those who are overwhelmed by anxieties? A Moonie does not have to think independently. Responsibility and worry are removed.

How do people find their way into the cult? Are they brainwashed during the recruiting period, as many parents and ex-Moonies claim?

Suppose you decide to attend a workshop after talking with a recruiter who visited the campus of your high school or college. What do you have to lose? The experience should be interesting; you may find out the truth about what happens to converts if you accept the invitation.

The weekend begins Friday night at a townhouse with a simple dinner: peanut-butter sandwich, some rather dry cheese, canned baked beans, a cucumber sandwich, and canned plums. The food at the building that houses the weekend workshop is not much different, but you did not attend for a gourmet feast. Before bedtime the first night, you sing hymns, play a few children's games, and pray. You sleep in a dormitory with several other potential recruits and several female members of the group who are constantly with you. Male members have separate quarters.

There is much action throughout the three-day weekend; so much that you are almost in a state of exhaustion. Every minute of each day is programmed. After an early rising, there are hymns, prayers, and exercises. Then comes breakfast, more hymns, and a lecture. A hymn follows this, and then another lecture with emphasis on the sins of the world and the one big family of Dr. Moon's followers who have rejected Satan, the forces of evil, and accepted the forces of good. The rest of the day is filled with more hymns, praying, more lectures, some simple games, still more praying, and a great deal of emphasis on the family's affection and group spirit. You are frequently made aware of the fact that Satan is out there in the world and that he is very clever. Brothers and sisters, as the family members are called, show absolute devotion to the group and a strong will to conform. You find yourself enjoying the feeling that you are accepted by the family, even wanted desperately by them. The prayers to save you are fervent. There are prayers to Father Moon asking for help and strength to understand his teaching. You are free to leave at the end of the workshop, but by then you may be in a state of confusion from the programmed action, the lack of sleep, the simple bland menus, and the cajolery and other techniques used by family members to try to get you to stay.

If you decide to visit the buildings at the upstate New York training center, you can see what your life would be like if you decided to join the family. Here, in a former Catholic seminary building complex that was purchased for $1,500,000, hymns, lectures, and prayers make up part of a day's program. As in other centers, male and female family members sit on separate sides of the hall even when attending lectures. The sex life is not the kind that most parents would frown upon, since chastity must continue even after marriage vows have been exchanged. The program leaves little time for contacting anyone outside the Moon-community or Moon-family. New recruits reach their moment of decision on whether to join the group after a period of activities that include seemingly endless lectures, prayer, and affection from the group. Some people join on a full-time basis, while others go back to their schools or work and contribute evenings and weekends to the work of the cult.

Why do parents complain about the Unification Church? Doing good work for a church in a drug-free atmosphere would please most parents. But many whose children have joined the Unification Church claim that their young have been spirited away from their families by brainwashing. Certainly, the programmed recruiting sessions seem to involve some of the characteristics common to the thought reform of political prisoners, but the conditions of force and captivity do not apply—unless one considers psychological conditioning a force.

The new Moonies are so busy with the program that they have little or no time for parents, old friends, and activities that once filled their lives. Members who receive letters from home suggesting or begging that they drop out of the movement are told that people who oppose the church are acting in behalf of Satan. Fear of Satan is one factor that may help to make members captives. Their total commitment is probably a combination of many factors. Some members claim that it has brought them a certain peace not found in the materialistic world.

Recently, a college class on contemporary legal problems invited a lawyer whose daughter had entered the Unification Church family to debate with a director of the group. The subject was whether or not the Unification Church used brainwashing or mind-capturing techniques in recruiting its members and in holding them. The father contended that the faith is dangerous because it robs an individual of control over his/her own mind. The church representative denied that the indoctrination process involved brainwashing. He claimed that the Moonies' unusual devotion was based on inspiring new vision and hope that caused their hearts to overflow with God's love and concern for their fellow man. This particular debate solved little because of the high degree of emotionalism of its participants.

Hundreds of parents and ex-converts from this and other cults have joined together to encourage federal government officials to investigate some of the cults that appear to them to have brainwashed young people. In February 1976, concerned people from various parts of the United States met in Washington, D.C. There Rabbi Maurice Davis of White Plains, New York, denounced the Moon group for creating suspicion against parents and hatred of those on the outside. Others, such as Dr. George W. Swope, professor of psychology and sociology at Westchester Community College in New York, read passages from a purported training manual for teachers in the movement. Among other things, Dr. Moon was quoted as saying: "The whole world is in my hand and I will conquer and subjugate the world."

At the meeting mentioned above, some ex-converts testified that they were taught justification in "deceiving Satan's children" in a doctrine known as "heavenly deception." At other occasions, ex-converts testified that they had been exposed to periods of little sleep, nonstop indoctrination, and emotional confusion during training for their work in Moon's sect. One girl testified before a Vermont State Judiciary Committee in March 1976 that her mind was controlled. She reported the use of isolation and a lot of physical fatigue that accomplished mind control in a very subtle fashion.

A Harvard psychiatrist, Dr. John Clark, Jr., recently testified in the District of Columbia Superior Court that he had examined ex-Moonies who seemed physically and emotionally exhausted. Others who have known converts say that they serve the group as if they were slaves. This is particularly galling to some parents and other outsiders as they believe the leaders are living in luxury. One aspect of the workshops and recruiting techniques that frightens parents is the psychological coercion apparently used to keep members from leaving the group when they develop doubts.

The following is quoted from an article by Paul Engel, an ex-Moonie, in which he details his personal experiences in the Unification Church.

> I have experienced a world in which there are no individuals but only a mass of obedient, non-thinking robots doing the will of one man whom they believe to

be the Messiah, the Second Coming of Christ, in essence, God himself. The future world of George Orwell, Aldous Huxley, and B. F. Skinner are present realities. It exists in the many destructive cults of today.

I was a member of one such cult, the Unification Church headed by "Reverend" Sun Myung Moon. It has many names—over forty different front organizations. Some of them are One World Crusade, Freedom Leadership Foundation, C.A.R.P. (Collegiate Association for the Research of Principles), and New Education Development, to name a few. It was this last, N.E.D., under which I entered the movement. Since that time in May, 1975, it has changed its name again. All these names are innocuous, academic sounding fronts for a movement whose goal is to take over the world and set up "Reverend" Moon as the sole authority.

You may wonder how any thinking person could become involved in such an organization. First of all, I was totally ignorant about these kinds of movements and the techniques used to get people to join. Moreover, I had lost faith in myself, other people, and the world as a potentially good place. I was a college graduate traveling with no definite direction, disillusioned about personal relationships, and alienated from the world. . . .

. . . I am deeply grateful to be out of a situation where others were controlling my mind and my life, and were trying to destroy my love for my family, friends, and the world. I believe it is important to do everything possible to keep others from being held captive and being used as I was. Please do not underestimate the power of "Reverend" Moon and his Church.*

In August 1975 a group known as Citizens Engaged in Reuniting Families was formed by families of "young men and women who have been caught up in the Unification Church." Young people who have been rescued from the church are also members of this group. While they do not participate in rescuing young people, deprogramming them, or any activities that they feel may violate the civil rights of Moon or his church, they do offer advice on how parents can best communicate with their sons and daughters in the movement. They have a legal staff that offers them advice, they keep parents informed of the activities of the Moon Group, counsel young people who have left the movement, supply information to the media, and perform many other functions. For further information about this group, contact Rabbi Maurice Davis, P.O. Box 112H, Scarsdale, New York 10583.

Citizens Engaged in Reuniting Families is only one of several similar groups relating to the Unification Church and several thousand other cults. Some of the others follow: Committee Engaged in Freeing Minds, P.O. Box 5084, Arlington, Texas 70611; Citizens Freedom Foundation, P.O. Box 256, Chula Vista, California 92012; and Individual Freedom Foundation, P.O. Box 48, Ardmore, Pennsylvania 19072.

*Quoted with permission.

Another of the popular movements being questioned about methods of recruiting and keeping followers is known as the Children of God. According to the beliefs of the Children of God, and of some of the other groups, the end of the world will soon come. Signs are everywhere. For example, many world leaders have failed. The number of earthquakes has increased. The second nation of Israel has already come as prophesied. The blazing comet, Kohouteck, came to warn of the end of the world. Those who join the group will be ready for the end of the world.

A former member of the Children of God group reports that the mind control or brainwashing used on him was a slow, scarcely recognizable process that involved the twisting of old truths. In an atmosphere of friendly and smiling people, he was exposed to suggestion while in a prayerful and meditative state. He believes that the smiling group members who talked with him were already converted through a process of mind control and that they believed completely that they were doing a righteous thing.

Members of the Children of God provided smooth and confident answers to all the questions that this young man raised. Their loving attitude helped to make tricky and questionable statements sound convincing. Trainees are reportedly exposed to interpretations of the Bible out of context. For example, one of the favorites used to help alienate trainees from family and friends is the out-of-context use of Matthew 10:36:

"And a man's enemies will be members of his household." By interpreting scriptures in such a way that they persuade the convert to believe that the devil works strongest on those close to him/her in order to destroy his/her faith, the recruiters accomplish a mistrust of those relatives and friends who encourage the person to leave the cult. According to ex-members, the close scrutiny of the "spiritual leaders" gives members little opportunity to express fears and doubts.

If one can be convinced that his/her own mind cannot be trusted, and if one can be told often enough that any doubts and longings are the work of the devil, complete alienation from former supportive individuals may be accomplished. Along with the constant propounding of the cult's beliefs, an element of fear is reportedly introduced, so that even though the converts are told they are free to leave, few do so.

A mission of the Children of God is to convert stragglers to their group, a worldwide network of colonies with thousands and thousands of members headed by Moses David or "Mo." Members pass out literature about the group, meeting quotas such as two thousand pieces of literature sold at ten cents apiece each week. Money goes to the Children of God activities. Each member has forsaken his/her own possessions, original family, and friends and has pledged allegiance to leaders who have convinced him/her that leaving the new family means going to hell.

Perhaps it is less important to determine whether or not these people have been brainwashed or subjected to some form of severe mind control than whether or not the experience is harmful to them. Parents who report that their children seem dazed, speak strangely, smile with mechanical smiles, and show no emotion other than fear feel that such conditioning is harmful. Some parents have hired a man, Ted Patrick, to "deprogram" their sons and daughters. He claims to have rescued over a thousand youths from religious-oriented cults.

According to psychologists, "brainwashing" can work both ways. The same methods of isolation, dependency, and duress can be used to persuade an individual to *reverse* his/her attitudes and beliefs. According to Dr. James Chaplin, professor of psychology at St. Michael's College in Vermont, the highly emotional brainwashed state requires reinforcement by other members of the group. Programmers play upon vulnerable features of an individual's personality and make him/her feel important, needed, and involved. But the same methods used in programming for cult membership can be used to deprogram.

Many parents take comfort in the studies indicating that brainwashing or thought control is not necessarily successful over a long period of time. If the young people who join the cults are under a form of mind control, the destruction of normal patterns of living and total disorientation will probably not be permanent. Even the relatively few American prisoners of war who were successfully brainwashed to communism in the Far East were successfully deprogrammed.

Those who join the Hare Krishna sect as adolescents may well go back to their old life-styles, too, if they are taken out of the environment that has encouraged their devotion to it. Hare Krishna members in the United States total about five thousand. Like the members of the Unification Church and the Children of God, they are organized as devoted fund raisers. They are also insulated from the outside world, and they give up their possessions and old family ties when they take on their new identities. Most Krishna devotees take Indian-style names and serve their Lord with great devotion.

Disciples of the International Society for Krishna-Consciousness send their children to school in Dallas, Texas, at an early age. Here, at Gurukula, they are steeped in ancient Hindu doctrine. The effects of mind control at such an early age may be more powerful than at a later age.

You may have seen Krishna devotees selling incense and books on the streets of a city someplace in the United States. They were once easily recognized by their orange costumes and shaven heads with topknots of hair called *sikas*. Sikas are believed to "help hoist to heaven." Recently, members of the sect have been seen in clothing that does not identify them. Their new attire, which in some cases includes toupees, helps them to "educate the outside world" by distributing their Hare Krishna magazine in camouflage. The spiritual masters of this group claim to be direct descendants of Lord Krishna, whose life story varies, but whose cult became widespread in India probably toward the close of the fifteenth century. Members believe that Krishna, the "Supreme Personality of Godhead," resides in every spirit and that all spirits, but not bodies, are equal. By selfless concentration on the presence of Krishna by the chanting of the Hare Krishna mantra 1,728 times a day, and denial of all material and some other gratifications, one can be liberated from the cycle of death and rebirth and its accompanying problems of disease and aging. One can thus be elevated to eternity with Lord Krishna in the spiritual sky. The life-style is complex, austere, and dedicated. The young raised in this sect know only this world and do not question whether their minds are being controlled by submission to leaders and their doctrines.

Just a few of the more popular cults that are currently popular have been mentioned. Every religion and every culture makes use of some of the psychological aspects of group sanctions, guilt, shame, reward, and so on, but these are limited in most cases to allow a balance that enables individuals to retain their freedom and creativity.

For some people, joining cults appears to be a fair exchange for freedom from the problems and anxieties of the materialistic world. On the other hand, many ex-cultists feel that they were brainwashed into slavery. Were they subjected to a form of behavior modification? Were they conditioned to accept a new life-style for their own benefit or for others'? Perhaps you want to provide your own answers. Or perhaps you feel that each individual case is different.

10 MEDITATION AND OTHER ALTERED STATES

■ Many forms of mind control involve altering states of consciousness. Some altered states have already been mentioned in this book. They include hypnosis, dreaming, trance, ecstasy, and others. If one considers the normal state of consciousness to be the state in which most waking hours are spent, altered states may be defined as any states other than normal. *Consciousness* is difficult to define since it has many individual aspects. For some people, a trance state may be their normal condition for most waking hours. But generally, one might consider altered states of consciousness as those in which an individual feels a certain shift of quality in the pattern of mental functioning and in which some quality or many qualities of his/her mental processes are different.

Meditation, a form of mind control over one's body, has become a very popular altered state of consciousness. This form of self-regulation has been practiced in India and other countries for many hundreds of years, but its daily use in the lives of large numbers of people in the Western world is recent. While it still varies greatly from time to time and from place to place, the most popular form in the United States at present is Transcendental Meditation (TM).

Meditation is sometimes defined as a state in which one thinks of nothing, a sort of clearing of the mind. Actually, it may be an attempt to increase or decrease awareness. In one type of meditation, there is a deliberate attempt to increase awareness of the external environment. For example, a form of Yoga called "The Witness" uses an exercise in which one attempts to observe self as if one were another person. The observation is not to be critical or to attempt change, but is an attempt to increase awareness of self. In some techniques of meditation in which there is an attempt to increase awareness, the present is observed as against the past or future.

Meditation can also restrict awareness to a single process and withdraw attention from ordinary thought processes. This may be done in a wide variety of ways. For example, Eskimos sometimes meditate by sitting in front of a large, soft stone, carving a circle in the soft stone with a hard stone, carving circles within circles, for what may be several days. A trance state often results.

In his popular book, *The Psychology of Conscious-ness*, Dr. Robert E. Ornstein describes meditation among the Bushmen of the Kalahari Desert in Africa. These people dance in a circle around a fire with their eyes on the fire, which provides a fixed focus point of concentration. In addition to the continuous dancing, the Bushmen chant repetitiously.

Whether a chant is repeated again and again or one stares at the fire, the sun, a candle, or another object, the physiological effect is much the same. Early Christians, and some modern ones, meditate while staring at the crucified figure of Christ on the cross, or at the cross alone. The popular object of concentration for Taoists is the abdomen. The repetitive whirl of the famous dervishes is a form of meditation. All these experiences restrict the awareness to one single process and withdraw attention from ordinary thought processes. Dr. Ornstein suggests that meditation might be considered psychologically as an attempt to recycle the same substance over and over in the nervous system.

The turning-off of perception as a form of meditation has been used for centuries in so many ways that descriptions fill the pages of many books. Why, then, is there so much current excitement about Transcendental Meditation, especially in the Western world?

After TM was introduced to the United States by Maharishi Mahesh Yogi in 1959, so many people found it helpful that they spread the word to their friends. By the 1970s, hundreds of thousands of people had taken courses that taught them the technique. Who is Maharishi Mahesh Yogi? He is a monk who was born in India, graduated with a degree in physics from Allahabad University, and is a disciple of "Guru Dev," formerly one of the four main spiritual leaders of India. Maharishi studied with his teacher for thirteen years. When Guru Dev was about to die, he charged his student with teaching laymen around the world a simple way to meditate. After going into seclusion in the Himalayas for two years, Maharishi came into the public eye with his technique for meditation. In 1956, he took the name *Maharishi*, which means "Great Seer" in Sanskrit. The popularity of TM has spread through the Western world to such a degree that a university in Fairfield, Iowa, is named Maharishi International University. Several books tell about the movement, and some of them have been bestsellers. Hundreds of TM centers have sprung up throughout the United States, Canada, and other countries. Along with other evidences of widespread interest, many people have referred to the technique as the spiritual survival kit of the present rootless generation. Others say that this drugless high replaces a drug turn-on. No matter how one views meditation, few argue against its benefits. Some say that it may be no better than just relaxing at regular intervals without the use of a mantra to "clear the mind"; but it does appear to ease tension without medication, alcohol, or other drugs. And it can be practiced anywhere, an advantage over many forms of exercise that also relieve stress.

Although Transcendental Meditation sounds mystical and is sometimes mistaken for a form of religion, it has nothing to do with philosophy or theology. Some people object to the cost of the program and others to the procedures, which include taking an "offering" to class in the form of a fresh, white handkerchief, a bunch of flowers, and several pieces of fresh fruit. These are accepted by the teacher and placed under a color portrait of Guru Dev on an altar with burning candles and incense. The teacher then chants in Sanskrit and gives the meditator his/her mantra, or sound on which to meditate. This mantra is chosen in accordance with a specific procedure. The meditator's birth date, temperament, life-style, profession, and other factors are said to enter into the selection of this sound, which has no meaning in English. Those who use the TM method to meditate promise to keep their mantras secret.

While most TM books encourage people to take the course, at least one advocate of meditation has written about how it can be done without taking the course. In *The Relaxation Response*, Dr. Herbert Benson suggests six simple rules for achieving the physiological benefits of practicing meditation, benefits that he has carefully researched in extensive studies conducted at Harvard's Thorndike Laboratory and at Boston's Beth Israel Hospital.

Transcendental Meditation (a name which has been patented) and the relaxation-response system described by Dr. Benson are part of what has been called a peaceful meditation war. Both approaches claim to help most people in a wide variety of ways. Many people who meditate regularly lower their blood pressure, sleep more restfully, consume less oxygen during meditation, become less dependent on cigarettes, alcohol, and other drugs, and show an increase in alpha waves in the brain during meditation. Since alpha waves are not fully understood, one cannot assume that this is a medical benefit, but an increase does appear to accompany a feeling of relaxation.

Meditators using either of the above techniques or other approaches claim that they have increased amounts of energy after their experiences with this form of mind control.

Even for those who meditate, the degree of self-regulation varies widely. Some areas of mind control present people with problems to explore; other areas suggest possibilities to suspect and fear. It has much to offer those people who need help, though they must have the right, scientifically qualified help.

The kinds of mind control are so numerous and far-reaching that it would take many volumes for a complete discussion of them. We have limited ourselves mainly to the kinds of mind control that are especially popular at the present time, especially bewildering for many individuals, or that affect large numbers of people. For anyone interested in further information about the types in this book or about other mind control techniques, the suggestions for further reading on the following pages should be helpful.

From the subtle forms of mind control to the obvious, much depends on the recognition and knowledge of the subject involved. Hopefully, education will increase the amount of *self* involved and decrease the fear of "Big Brother." Knowing about mind control can help you to be in control of your own mind.

SUGGESTIONS FOR
FURTHER READING

Bailey, Ronald H. *The Role of the Brain.* New York: Time-Life Books, 1975.

Bandura, A. *Principles of Behavior Modification.* New York: Holt, Rinehart and Winston, 1969.

Benson, Herbert. *The Relaxation Response.* New York: William Morrow, 1975.

Bloomfield, Harold H., Michael P. Cain, and Dennis T. Jaffe. *TM: Discovering Inner Energy and Overcoming Stress.* New York: Delacorte Press, 1975.

Brecher, Edward, ed. *The Consumers Union Report: Licit and Illicit Drugs.* Boston: Little, Brown, 1972.

Carpenter, Finley. *The Skinner Primer.* New York: The Free Press, 1974.

Condon, Richard. *The Manchurian Candidate.* New York: McGraw-Hill, 1959; New York: Dell, 1974.

Delgado, Jose M. R. *Physical Control of the Mind.* New York: Harper and Row, 1969.

Denniston, Denise, and Peter McWilliams. *The TM Book.* New York: Warner Books, 1975.

Evans, Wayne, and Nathan S. Kline. *Psychotropic Drugs in the Year 2000.* Springfield, Illinois: Charles C. Thomas, 1971.

Feshback, Seymour, and Robert D. Singer. *Television and Aggression.* San Francisco: Jossey-Bass, 1971.

Frank, Jerome. *Persuasion and Healing.* New York: Schocken Books, 1974.

Gaylin, Willard M., Joe S. Meister, and Robert C. Neville. *Operating on the Mind.* New York: Basic Books, 1976.

Graziano, Anthony. *Behavior Therapy with Children,* Vol. II. Chicago: Aldine Publishing Company, 1975.

Hemingway, Patricia Drake. *The Transcendental Meditation Primer.* New York. David McKay, 1975.

Hilts, Philip J. *Behavior Mod.* New York: Harper's Magazine Press, 1974.

Hyde, Margaret O. *Mind Drugs,* Third Edition. New York: McGraw-Hill, 1974.

————., Edward S. Marks, and J. Wells. *Mysteries of the Mind.* New York: McGraw-Hill, 1972.

————. *Your Brain: Master Computer.* New York: McGraw-Hill, 1964.

Lifton, Robert Jay. *Thought Reform and the Psychology of Totalism: A Study of Brainwashing in China.* New York: Norton 1969.

London, Perry. *Behavior Control.* New York: Harper and Row, 1969.

Mark, Vernon, and Frank Ervin. *Violence and the Brain.* New York: Harper and Row, 1970.

Meerloo, Joost A. M. *The Rape of the Mind.* New York: Grosset and Dunlap, 1961.

Mitford, Jessica. *Kind and Unusual Punishment.* New York: Knopf, 1973.

Nolen, William A. *Healing: A Doctor in Search of a Miracle.* New York: Random House, 1974.

Ornstein, Robert E. *The Psychology of Consciousness.* New York: Viking Press, 1972.

Orwell, George. *1984.* New York: Harcourt Brace Jovanovich, 1959.

Packard, Vance. *The Hidden Persuaders.* New York: Pocket Books, 1958.

Patrick, Ted. *Let Our Children Go!* New York: Dutton, 1976.

Penfield, Wilder. *The Mystery of the Mind.* Princeton, New Jersey: Princeton University Press, 1975.

Pizzat, Frank. *Behavior Modification in Residential Treatment for Children.* New York: Behavioral Publications, 1973.

Pines, Maya. *The Brain Changers: Scientists and the New Mind Control.* New York: Harcourt Brace Jovanovich, 1973.

Rose, Steven. *The Conscious Brain.* New York: Knopf, 1973.

Sarason, Irwin G., Edward M. Glaser, and George A. Fargo. *Reinforcing Productive Classroom Behavior.* New York: Behavioral Publications, 1972.

Schiller, Herbert I. *The Mind Managers.* Boston: Beacon Press, 1973.

Skinner, B. F. *Beyond Freedom and Dignity.* New York: Knopf, 1971.

———. *Science and Human Behavior.* New York: The Free Press, 1965.

———. *Walden Two.* New York: Macmillan, 1956.

Tart, Charles, ed. *Altered States of Consciousness.* New York: John Wiley and Sons, 1969.

Smith, Adam. *Powers of Mind.* New York: Random House, 1975.

Ulrich, Roger, Thomas Stachick, and John Mabry. *Control of Human Behavior.* Glenview, Illinois: Scott, Foresman, 1974.

Valenstein, Eliot. *Brain Control: A Critical Examination of Brain Stimulation and Psychosurgery.* New York: Wiley Interscience, 1973.

Wolberg, Lewis R. *Hypnosis.* New York: Harcourt Brace Jovanovich, 1972.

Wolpe, Joseph. *The Practice of Behavior Therapy.* New York: Pergamon Press, 1973.

Yates, Aubrey J. *Behavior Therapy.* New York: John Wiley and Sons, 1970.

GLOSSARY

Addiction. An obsession or compelling craving for something, such as alcohol, other drugs or certain conditions or activities.

Alpha waves. The brain rhythm that is predominant in certain relaxed states of feeling.

Animal magnetism. Theory of F. A. Mesmer; the hypothetical force which induces hypnosis by being transferred from the hypnotist to the subject.

Autism. Tendency for withdrawal from real life more or less equivalent to extreme wishful thinking and daydreaming.

Autogenic training. A form of medical therapy based on specially prescribed physical and mental exercises.

Aversion therapy. One in which unwanted behavior is

stopped through use of an unpleasant situation which associates negative reactions to the behavior normally enjoyed.

Behavior modification. Projects designed to predict, control and modify human behavior. Any learned response to any stimulas.

Beta waves. Pattern of brain waves predominant when a person is mentally active.

Biofeedback. Form of mind control whereby certain involuntary processes in the body can be controlled voluntarily.

Brainwashing. Forcible application of prolonged and intensive indoctrination sometimes including mental torture in an attempt to induce someone to give up basic political, social, or religious beliefs and attitudes and to accept contrasting ideas.

Cerebellum. Part of the human brain primarily concerned with coordinating muscular activity so that motions are smooth and precise.

Cerebral cortex. Part of the human brain which enables a person to think, reason and to use language.

Classical conditioning. Occurs when a conditioned stimulus is paired with an unconditioned stimulus. Also known as *Pavlovian conditioning.*

Coercive persuasion. Gaining or forcing compliance through belief or faith.

Conditioned reflex. Originated by I. P. Pavlov; any response aroused by a stimulus other than the natural one.

Conditioned stimulus. Through classical conditioning has become an effective stimulus for a response which was originally caused by another [unconditioned] stimulus.

Delta waves. The brain rhythm that is predominant during sleep.

Extra sensory perception (ESP). Awareness of an external event which is not conveyed by any of the known senses.

Frontal lobotomy. An operation on the frontal part of the brain resulting in a radical personality change.

Hypnosis. State of heightened suggestibility induced by another person or by oneself usually involving bodily relaxation and concentration on a narrow range of stimuli.

Hypnotherapy. Hypnosis combined with psychological treatment to relieve symptoms and to help in an understanding of the reasons for them.

Hypothalamus. One of the two areas of the human brain, located above the brain stem and under the cerebral hemispheres. It regulates body temperature, eating, drinking and sexual behavior and emotions.

In vivo flooding. Technique whereby a patient with a feared situation is actually put into that situation in the presence of the therapist.

Limbic system. Located above the reptilian brain, and part of the human brain, this thick, doughnut-shaped mass controlling mood or emotional changes ranging from euphoria to violence is effected by stimuli. Also known as the *mammalian brain.*

Mantra. A ritualistic incantation or mystic formula used devotionally in popular Hinduism, and more recently, in different religious cults.

Meditation. A spiritual exercise consisting in deep continued reflection on a specific theme which may result in changing the rate of certain body processes.

Mesmerism. Originated by Franz Mesmer; obsolete term for hypnotism.

Mood drugs (legal). The caffeine in coffee, tea, cola drinks, chocolate; cigarettes and alcohol.

Motor nerve. See nerve pathways.

Nerve pathways. Consists of two kinds: sensory and motor. For example, the sensory nerves carry messages causing the motor nerves to flash their commands of appropriate muscles.

Neurons. Over 13,000 million nerve cells in the brain using a system of frequency of impulses in each burst which tells the next cell about the strength of the signal.

Observational learning. A technique in behavior modification using a variation of systematic densensitization to help people overcome phobias. Also known as *modeling.*

Operant conditioning. A form of behavior modification where behavior is changed by manipulating the consequences of every act through rewards and punishments.

Phobias. Deep-seated fears that may be symptoms of some deeply buried problems.

Phrenology. A psuedo-science developed by Francis Gall (1800s) analyzing the bumps on a human skull.

Psychosurgery. The destruction or stimulation of parts of the brain through the use of surgery, radiation, or other techniques in an effort to alter the patient's behavior.

Reptilian brain. The lowest inside layer of a human brain consisting mainly of the brain stem and a part called the midbrain.

Reticular activating system (RAS). A kind of filter or monitor for all the messages that your senses receive.

Sedative neurosurgery. A form of surgery to eliminate dangerous behavior through assault. It destroys tissues in extremely small areas of the limbic brain.

Sensory nerve. See nerve pathways.

Shame therapy. A form of behavior modification where unwanted behavior is discussed by a group in the presence of the person who has come for help.

Stress. A condition of physical or mental strain which produces changes in the autonomic nervous system.

Systematic desensitization. A technique of behavior therapy using a stimulus which is presented repeatedly in small but increasing doses while the patient is relaxed, decreasing the fear until it becomes more realistic.

Transcendental meditation (TM). A simple technique of meditation introduced in 1959 by Maharishi Mahesh Yogi, involving ritual offerings, mantras, and faithful practice.

Thalamus. One of two small areas in the brain lying under the cerebral hemispheres and above the brain stem, serving as a switchboard to which all the sensory information the body receives is relayed.

Theta waves. The pattern of brain waves most prevalent in the stage of consciousness reached just before sleep.

Token economy. Technique of behavior modification by which behavior to be changed is spelled out step by step and rewards are a form of token which may be exchanged for a desired activity or thing.

Unconditioned stimulus. Evokes an unconditioned response without prior learning or conditioning and may serve as a reinforcing agent.

INDEX